Excellence in Public Discourse

John Stuart Mill, John Dewey, and Social Intelligence

THE JOHN DEWEY LECTURE

The John Dewey Lecture is delivered annually under the sponsorship of the John Dewey Society. This book is an elaboration of the Lecture given in 1983. The intention of the series is to provide a setting where able thinkers from various sectors of our intellectual life can direct their most searching thought to problems that involve the relation of education to culture. Arrangements for the presentation of the Lecture and its publication by Teachers College Press are under the direction of the John Dewey Society Lecture Commission, D. Bob Gowin, Chairperson.

Excellence in Public Discourse

John Stuart Mill, John Dewey, and Social Intelligence

JAMES GOUINLOCK
Emory University

TEACHERS
COLLEGE
PRESS

Teachers College, Columbia University
New York and London

Published by Teachers College Press, 1234 Amsterdam Avenue, New York, N.Y. 10027

Library of Congress Cataloging-in-Publication Data

Gouinlock, James.
  Excellence in public discourse.

  (The John Dewey lecture ;   )
  Bibliography: p.
  Includes index.
  1. Educational sociology.   2.   Mill, John Stuart,
1806–1873—Views on freedom of speech.   3.   Dewey, John,
1859–1952—Views on freedom of speech.   4.   Education—
Philosophy.   I.   Title.   II.   Series.
LC189.G65   1986   370.19   86-14582

ISBN 0-8077-2825-X

Manufactured in the United States of America

91 90 89 88 87 86   1 2 3 4 5 6

Dedicated to
Michael DeSisto, Mitch Kosh, Sharon Dockter,
the entire faculty and staff of the DeSisto Schools,
and Helen Hafner,
who are as devoted to the flourishing of youth as were
John Stuart Mill and John Dewey

Contents

Foreword

Classical liberalism, celebrating laissez-faire individualism and free-dom from governmental interference, is associated with the nine-teenth-century English philosopher, John Stuart Mill. Pragmatic liberalism, celebrating the social as the context for empowered in-dividuality, is associated with the ideals of creative democracy and the philosopher, John Dewey, of nineteenth- and twentieth-century America. Central to liberalism and liberty is the notion of free speech in a public space. If such social discourse is silenced, the individual has no freedom of thought. Participation in social intercourse, as free and fluent as it may become, supports the creation of individuality and the consequent underpinnings of democracy. In this freshly minted book by James Gouinlock, we are presented with important new insights from both Mill and Dewey, an incisive interpretation of their texts, and some refreshing ways to view social inquiry into the important and unresolved, deeply conflicting issues of our time.

Inquiry into social conflicts, to be fair and effective, must let all things be considered. Political tags of "liberal," "conservative," "radical," and "reactionary" are not concepts that help clarify genu-ine social inquiry. These tags do indicate the *fact* of passionate con-cern, intense debate, unsettled beliefs. This fact is what social in-telligence begins with: Something is *problematic;* the solution is therefore not yet known. Moreover, in the heat of dispute the con-cepts and procedures of social inquiry seem hard to come by. Both Mill and Dewey understood this fact, and they both provided us with theories and methods to render the indeterminate more determinate. Dewey felt strongly that doubt and disturbance could be converted into consummatory satisfactions by instituting social intelligence. *Social intelligence becomes the basis for excellence in public discourse.*

In a media-rich society such as ours today, radio and television "talk shows" give the appearance of public discourse. But often these journalistic displays emphasize entertainment over edification, and serve to silence genuine social inquiry.

Mill constructed an argument about why we should not silence free speech. He argued, in effect, that if the silenced opinion turns out to be true, then people are deprived of the chance to exchange error for truth; and if, on the other hand, silenced opinion is wrong, then people are deprived of the chance to experience the value of truth winning out over error. In both cases, silencing means that educating can lose its energy. In democratic societies, educating plays a truly significant role. The relationship between education and the continuity of culture is most important. We cannot simply rely on handed-down solutions, because those are not the solutions to current and novel problems. Each generation must do its thinking for itself. It is a credit to Professor Gouinlock's book that he is able to winnow out previously important problems-and-solutions (which are irrelevant to today's issues), in order to make explicit central meanings useful for contemporary thought. The power for free speech helps identify problems, and it helps to educate a public to see the difference between mere "talk" and excellence in public discourse.

Who, specifically, could benefit from reading this book? What is the audience? Social philosophers and philosophers of education are a primary audience. The book also will appeal to a wide audience of intelligent lay readers and dedicated educational professionals. As an educator myself, I am keenly interested in the contributions the book makes to curriculum, to learners learning, to teachers teaching, to large issues of educational governance. In my view, educating about the social in high schools, colleges, and research universities could be much improved by wide use of this book. It seems a great pity to me that studies of social events are so often uninformed by the greatest social thinkers in the Western tradition. High school social studies can add this book to their curriculum. Collegiate social sciences can better prepare their undergraduates by integrating the philosophic with the scientific. Graduate programs of social research will find new and generative questions arising from thoughtful pondering of these ideas. Admittedly, these texts are difficult; yet they are also illuminating. While difficult to study, they reward hard work because as students begin to grasp the meaning of these ideas, they begin to see more with less, they experience the value of broad and meaningful connection-making. They also begin to feel more at home with perplexities, and consequently more empowered to face current problems that can neither be solved nor abandoned.

One aim of the John Dewey Society is to sponsor lectures, discussions, and publication of scholarship that considers the rich interaction of culture and education. This book makes a noteworthy contribution to that aim.

* * * * *

The John Dewey Society annually sponsors the John Dewey Society Lecture. Professor Gouinlock gave the lecture for 1983 in Detroit, Michigan, before an audience of professional educators gathered to exchange views of both the excellence and the future of schools and other educational institutions. His book is a significant expansion on that lecture. The expansion includes telling selections from the original writings of John Stuart Mill and John Dewey, bringing together for the first time key ideas of social intelligence widely scattered in the corpus of Dewey's work.

D. BOB GOWIN
Professor of Foundations of Education,
Cornell University,
Chair, John Dewey Society Lecture Commission

Acknowledgments

I am grateful to the officers of the John Dewey Society for honoring me with the invitation to give the John Dewey Lecture for 1983. I also wish to thank them and the members of the Society for their courtesy and good company on the occasion of my delivering the Lecture in February of that year. I applaud the Society for its efforts to carry on the spirit of John Dewey's thought and action, and I hope that the present work makes its own contribution to their cause.

I am indebted to my colleague at Emory, Donald Verene, for his very helpful suggestions when I was still in the phase of wondering what the subject matter for the lecture and subsequent monograph should be. Once I had found some direction in the way of a topic, I benefited greatly from continued conversations with D. Bob Gowin. His advice and encouragement have been most helpful, and much appreciated, throughout the preparation of this volume.

Jo Ann Boydston, Director of the Center for Dewey Studies, has been extremely helpful. Her advice has made the production of this work not only simpler, but much more pleasant as well. My enthusiastic thanks to her.

It is a pleasure to thank Audrey Kingstrom and Peter Ross Sieger of Teachers College Press. Both have been tolerant, supportive, and helpful.

I also wish to express my gratitude to Emory University for providing me with a leave of absence during the fall semester of 1985, when this book was written.

Grateful acknowledgment is made to the following for permission to reprint materials from the works indicated:

From the series, *John Dewey, The Later Works, 1925-1953*, edited by Jo Ann Boydston: *The Public and Its Problems* (Vol. 2: 1925-1927); *The Quest for Certainty* (Vol. 4: 1929); *Individualism, Old and New* and "Three Independent Factors in Morals" (Vol. 5: 1929-1930); *Ethics* (Vol. 7: 1932). Volumes 2, 4, and 5 © 1984, volume 7 © 1985 by the Board of Trustees, Southern Illinois University. Reprinted by permission of Southern Illinois University Press.

The Putnam Publishing Group, for John Dewey, *Freedom and Culture,* © 1967 by Mrs. John Dewey; for John Dewey, *Liberalism and Social Action,* © 1962 by Roberta L. Dewey; and for John Dewey, "Creative Democracy—The Task Before Us," in Sidney Ratner (Ed.), *The Philosopher of the Common Man,* © 1968 by Horace M. Kallen.

Excellence in Public Discourse

John Stuart Mill, John Dewey, and Social Intelligence

CHAPTER 1

Introduction

Effective democracy requires excellence in public discourse. It requires excellence in our conversations concerning the ends and means of public life. Writers on democracy typically emphasize the importance of an informed citizenry, and their advice should be taken. Insofar as citizens determine public policy or decide who shall be the policy makers, at any level of government, it is important that they be familiar with the issues that they are called upon to address.

Excellence in public discourse requires more than this, however. Citizens must possess what Aristotle called moral and intellectual virtues. These are personal qualities of mind and character that are indispensable for carrying on associated life in a manner that is both voluntary and fulfilling. They make the difference between democracy as antagonistic rhetoric and democracy as the shared search for cooperative solutions.

If the discourse of our public life is lacking in these qualities, much of the responsibility must lie with those who presume to be leaders in such conversation. It is patronizing for educators, intellectuals, politicians, and members of the media to call for an intelligent public if they are complacent about the quality of their own participation in the democratic process. They might look for the beam in their own eye before wringing their hands about the mote in the eye of the public. The full study of excellence in democratic life would scrutinize those on whom we rely for defining and maintaining high standards of public debate and communication.

To determine the nature and conditions of excellence in popular government has been a central feature of the liberal tradition. In the

nineteenth century the greatest representative of this tradition was
John Stuart Mill; in the twentieth century it has been John Dewey.
Outside the coterie of professional philosophers, Mill is best remembered for his essay *On Liberty,* and especially for its second chapter,
"Of the Liberty of Thought and Discussion." This is one of the great
documents about public discourse. A superb case is made for freedom of speech. Mill promises great benefits from this freedom, and
he also provides an eloquent statement of the ethical behavior that is
required to make it a reality. One might easily believe that there is
little to be added to Mill's now-classic analysis.

Splendid though it is, it was found seriously deficient by Dewey.
Like Mill, Dewey was a multifaceted thinker, and he is recognized
above all as a philosopher of democracy. In the liberal tradition, the
sequel to Mill's elaboration of the meaning of free speech is Dewey's
theory of social intelligence. While Mill's argument can be found
largely in a single book, there is no comparable document in Dewey's
writings. His critique of the liberal tradition as he inherited it, and his
constructive additions to it, can be pieced together only by consulting
a variety of sources.

The present monograph will provide an exposition of Mill's position. It will also present Dewey's considerable reconstruction of it and
will provide additional analysis of issues in these philosophies that
are deserving of our attention. Finally, appendixes will provide a reprint of most of chapter II of *On Liberty* and a collection of excerpts
from a number of Dewey's works. The materials from Dewey as-
sembled in the appendix constitute the only source of his writings on
excellence in public discourse that can be found within the confines of
a single publication.

The search for the definition and conditions of effective democratic communication inevitably leads into such areas as philosophy
of mind, philosophy of science, and philosophy of education; and
these are the fields in which Dewey found Mill and the liberal tradition seriously wanting. We will find that Dewey's response to Mill
and classical liberalism contains trenchant criticism. It also misses
some of Mill's virtues and overlooks some of his problems—most
notably, a deep ambiguity in his conception of human nature and
hence in his philosophy of education. Dewey's theory of social intelligence will be set forth systematically. For all its power, it still has problems; but it is, I think, the best articulation in our literature of the
idea of democracy as a way of life.

The context of our inquiry is conspicuously practical. When we
wonder what constitutes excellence in public discourse and how to at-

tain it, we are not engaged in trifling matters. From virtually any author who addresses herself or himself to any phase of democratic life, we find statements to the effect that our characteristic practices and institutions are in a state of crisis. Perhaps it is the nature of democracy to be in perpetual crisis. There are always groups in anguish over the way other groups are trying to use the process to their own advantage; and the compliment is returned by the accused parties. Classic examples are the charges that the rich are subverting democracy for their own advantage or that disadvantaged classes are trying to use political action where economic action would be to their real benefit. We struggle over the question of what the responsibilities of democratic government ought to be. As the responsibilities are conceived more broadly, and the state becomes teacher, parent, entrepreneur, doctor, soldier, moralist, patron of the arts and sciences, and distributor of wealth, the greater the struggle becomes over how much the state ought to do, for whom, and at whose expense. The stakes in politics become extremely high. If the stakes are reduced, however, the outcries of injustice are multiplied. In a pluralistic society, rivalry and antagonism exist between competing interests, and a principal means of struggle between them is for each to try to use the political system to its particular benefit. Hence there are unceasing strains on the democratic process, and the assertions of claim and counterclaim readily become a Babel.

At the same time, it is part of the democratic ethic to sort out, understand, and assess such claims. We look for the truth and justice in them; and, if we are conscientious, we become advocates of the view that seems superior in these respects. As responsible participants, we feel obliged to hear all the claims relative to an issue upon which we intend to take a position. And we hear them out—we are not just going through the motions for the sake of appearances. It requires patience and understanding, and a fearful mass of information has to be digested. The privileges of living in a democratic society are matchless, but there are heavy demands as well.

The prospect is intimidating. Indeed, many students of politics and human nature have said that the task of democratic citizenship, if conceived in this way, is impossible. Mill, for example, believed that only an educated elite could be expected to perform such tasks and that the bulk of the voters had no recourse but to follow the advice of their mentors. (Mill, indeed, would give different weights to individual votes, varying with the demonstrated competence of the voter.) Dewey, on the other hand, held out greater hope for intelligent participation from the ordinary citizen. These are vexing issues, but at this point at least this can be said: If we are to have something more than a democracy in name only, then someone other than the politicians has to know what is going on. The larger that number, the better. No one, no matter how diligent and intelligent, can come close to mastering all the issues of contemporary politics. But on any given issue, our democracy is apt to be more vital and effective when a large, active, informed, and conscientious body of citizens is engaged with it.

As suggested earlier, the difficulty of being a democratic citizen is not just that of being adequately informed. The problem goes much deeper. There is also the need for a certain pervasive morale—a morale in which differences of aims and judgments will be tolerated and even respected, sincerely so. It is a matter of respect for persons. To the extent that this respect is lacking, the great and diverse groups in the nation see each other as threats and adversaries; they see themselves as engaged in a zero-sum game, rather than as participants groping for some kind of compatibility, trusting in a process of accommodation and growth. An underlying morale of public discourse is essential to maintain the social bonds in a democracy.

This morale is as precious as it is difficult to sustain. It is not something that can, or should, be legislated into existence. We do not want to have legal penalties affixed to the failure to take seriously the convictions of our fellow citizens. Yet we somehow want to bring this *esprit* into being. We have the intimation that it is essential if democracy is to rise above angry rhetoric and become truly constructive.

Under the stern demands of democratic discourse, it is all too easy to become by turns discouraged, apathetic, dogmatic, intolerant, and cynical. It is all too easy to succumb to the temptation to dismiss arguments out of hand. We read and hear only what reinforces our favorite beliefs. We become so enamored of a point of view that we smugly take it for granted that the evidence unfailingly supports it. We reassure ourselves that the people who hold opinions other than those of our own group are surely fools, probably crazy, and maybe wicked, too. They want to hand over the country to the communists; they want to oppress the poor; they want to plunge the country into war; they want to undermine the family. They are so prejudiced and corrupt that we can only think of them as enemies. Certainly they are beyond engagement in intelligent controversy. When we permit ourselves to think in this way, the virtues of public discourse can only languish. Sneers, taunts, and recrimination replace constructive argument.

Perhaps I am giving way to my worst fears, but I believe that discourse in the United States is in an alarming state of deterioration; it sorely needs critical analysis and reconstruction. Communication has become increasingly ill tempered, abusive, and dogmatic; the agencies responsible for nonpartisan inquiry and reporting are too readily engaged in distortion and special pleading. The intellectual class is smug and intolerant; its members speak with contempt not only for the opinions of the general public, but for those of each other as well. Some of those who would willfully silence another point of view, and sometimes do so, are some of those who pay homage to the memory of John Stuart Mill for his sterling defense of free speech.

When I first conceived of this book, I was tempted to make it a vehicle for a criticism of the nature of discourse in today's schools and universities and in the media, both popular and intellectual. I have resisted the temptation for several reasons. To avoid the use of merely anecdotal and biased evidence, I would have to engage in very extensive research. More importantly, the merits of the philosophies of Mill and Dewey have an enduring quality, and an appreciation of their ideas should not appear to be contingent upon practices that happen to be observed today. It is enough that students find here the pertinent ideas of John Stuart Mill and John Dewey and some analysis of their meaning.

As I have suggested, I see little evidence of the morale that distinguishes democratic discourse at its best; but perhaps my assessment of current conditions is overdrawn. In the present context, my foremost concern is that readers new to this subject will be stirred to some excitement and reflection by Mill and Dewey and will even be prompted to adopt new behavior. I trust also that scholars will find that my presentation brings some fresh insight, analysis, and order to this subject.

CHAPTER 2

Mill:
Knowledge and Moral Evaluation
as Social Products

Mill's discussion of freedom of speech is set in a broad moral context. Like most of Mill's writings, *On Liberty* is concerned with the emancipation and flourishing of the individual. It presents and defends a principle concerning the rightful limits of the intrusion of political and social forces into the lives of individuals, and it contains an analysis of the nature and conditions of human individuality. Chapter II, "Of the Liberty of Thought and Discussion," is in part an application of that principle; and it is also intended as an explication of one of the most important preconditions for the development of individuality.

He is careful to mention certain provisos to his defense of liberty. The most important of these assumes that the condition of freedom cannot be maintained in backward societies, where more authority is desirable. "Liberty, as a principle, has no application to any state of things anterior to the time when mankind have become capable of being improved by free and equal discussion" (Mill, 1859/1978, p. 10; hereinafter, references to *On Liberty* will be cited as *OL* in the text).

The moral ambitions of *On Liberty* are supported by Mill's ethical theory, a version of utilitarianism. This theory is not set forth explicitly, as it is in his volume, *Utilitarianism*; but it is assumed. Mill writes:

> It is proper to state that I forego any advantage which could be derived to my argument from the idea of abstract right as a thing independent of

> utility. I regard utility as the ultimate appeal on all ethical questions; but it must be utility in the largest sense, grounded on the permanent interests of man as a progressive being. (*OL*, p. 10)

Mill did not believe that government posed the greatest threat to freedom in mid–nineteenth-century England. He was, however, convinced we should never be complacent about the danger of state oppression, and he cautioned that it could occur in a democracy in the form of the tyranny of the majority over the minority. Nevertheless, he was far more concerned with the power of public opinion.

> Society can and does execute its own mandates; and if it issues wrong mandates instead of right, or any mandates at all in things with which it ought not to meddle, it practices a social tyranny more formidable than many kinds of political oppression, since, though not usually upheld by such extreme penalties, it leaves fewer means of escape, penetrating much more deeply into the details of life, and enslaving the soul itself. (*OL*, p. 4)[1]

Even when a person's behavior promises harm neither to himself nor to others, we have a strong tendency to demand that he behave as we think proper. We have our own ideas about what sort of lives other people ought to lead, and we demand that others conform to these concepts, like them or not. Antisocial behavior must be condemned and punished, Mill insists, but there is no justification for requiring individuals to adopt careers, personal habits, or traits of personality just because they are out of vogue with the rest of us. We may try by rational discussion to convince someone to alter his life-style, but we may not force him to do so; and so long as his conduct does no harm, we have no right to ridicule him or otherwise show lack of respect. The free development of individuality was not in Mill's judgment a luxury, but a great instrument of human progress.

A democratic society is not necessarily an impediment to the familiar habit of demanding social conformity. Indeed, it threatens to encourage it. Inspired both by his experience and by de Tocqueville's *Democracy in America*, Mill feared that the tendency of democratic culture is toward the acceptance of a kind of collective mediocrity and a hostility to individuality. Both the theory and practice of democratic life must remain alert to this threat.

Mill's analyses are not set in an exclusively moral context. There is an epistemological context as well. Sometimes the latter seems to predominate, but a thorough understanding of his arguments requires an appreciation of both. Mill himself moves insensibly from moral to epistemological considerations in his defense of freedom of speech. He sometimes offers arguments that appeal to the value of keen and diverse intellects to individual and social well-being. This is a moral argument. At other times he simply discusses the means of correcting errors and discovering truth, where the value of truth need not be at issue. Freedom of speech is essential to both goals. Mill believed that truth is crucially valuable to human welfare; so the merely epistemological arguments have moral import.

The remarks on the first few pages of chapter II, "Of the Liberty of Thought and Discussion," indicate that the first merit of freedom of speech consists in its being a means to truth. Mill regarded truth to be precious, but he nowhere addresses in a systematic way the question of the value of truth.[2] Why is truth valuable? Mill's answer, drawn from any number of sources and remarks, is clear. Possession of truth permits us to function as well as possible in our converse with all of the events of our experience. We act in relation to objects, persons, complex natural and social processes. If we are to act effectively with these things, whether we are well or ill motivated, we must know how *they* act; we must know their properties and behavior. We have to find out the nature of fire in order to utilize it for predictable and controllable consequences; likewise with lovers, libraries, government officials, or anything else. Two points might be distinguished here. First, in order to *achieve* our ends, we have to attain mastery of the means. Second, in order to *evaluate* ends, we must know not just the means, but the ends as well. Our evaluation of any sort of situation depends on our knowing somewhat about its nature. If one is evaluating the condition known as friendship, for example, he must know what it is that he is evaluating; he must know the typical qualities, functions, rights, and responsibilities that characterize that relationship. There is no need to wax mystical about Truth. It is simply that without knowing the truth about relevant events in our lives, our conduct would be helpless, impotent in the extreme. With the truth, we have a greater opportunity to enhance the quality of life.

Why is freedom of speech a means to truth? A remarkable feature of this chapter of *On Liberty* is Mill's assertion that we can have no confidence in the truth of a proposition until the claim in question has survived a *social* process. After stating that no individual is infallible, he says that empirical observation alone is not a sufficient test for ideas. What is necessary as well is that they be completely open to criticism from any and all persons. Only when an argument has been subjected to this social test can we be confident of its validity. It is worth quoting Mill at length. He writes:

When we consider either the history of opinion or the ordinary conduct of human life, to what is to be ascribed that the one and the other are no worse than they are? Not certainly to the inherent force of human understanding, for on any matter not self-evident there are ninety-nine persons incapable of judging it for one who is capable; and the capacity of the hundredth is only comparative, for the majority of the eminent men of every past generation held many opinions now known to be erroneous, and did or approved numerous things which no one will now justify. . . . [T]he source of everything respectable in man either as an intellectual or as a moral being . . . [is] that his errors are corrigible. He is capable of rectifying his mistakes by discussion and experience. . . . The whole strength and value, then, of human judgment depending on the one property, that it can be set right when it is wrong, reliance can be placed on it only when the means of setting it right are kept constantly at hand. . . .

The beliefs we have most warrant for have no safeguard to rest on but a standing invitation to the whole world to prove them unfounded. . . . [I]f the lists are kept open, we may hope that, if there be a better truth, it will be found when the human mind is capable of receiving it; and in the meantime we may rely on having attained such approach to truth as is possible in our own day. This is the amount of certainty attainable by a fallible being, and this is the sole way of attaining it. (*OL*, pp. 18–20)[a]

The individual mind is highly imperfect. It makes many mistakes. But we can correct our mistakes. The remedy for our deficiencies, Mill insists, cannot be reliance on the resources of the individual mind as such. It consists, rather, in dependence upon a process of criticism that we share with other persons. The remedy for the charms of superstition, prejudice, propaganda, and undisciplined speculation is not just in demanding the test of verification in experience. It consists as well in the willingness to share inquiry with others. Such publicity, as we shall see, does more than rescue us from various intellectual maladies. It calls forth intellectual excellence as well.

This claim is remarkable because it constitutes a radical change in classical empiricist epistemology. Mill's predecessors had all believed that a true belief is distinguished from a false one by, ultimately, the subjective quality of that belief. There is, they thought, a distinctive kind of personal feeling that accompanies true belief—a certain vivacity and persistence. Hence when one has that *feeling*, the belief is true.[3] But Mill is not using subjective criteria. He means that to know something is true, I must not rely on the subjective state of my own mind, but I must get a corroborating verdict from a number of other persons. His position leads to the view that we learn to judge an idea to be true if it has survived the appropriate testing, regardless of the subjective qualities of the idea. Mill did not seem to realize what a revolutionary step he took, and this idea is not repeated in his *System of Logic* (1872/1956). The notion that truth is a social product is normally attributed first to the pragmatist Charles Sanders Peirce[4]; but here it is indisputably in *On Liberty*.

Mill makes no effort to elaborate the point that warranted belief is the outcome of a social process. That is, he does not tell us much about the nature of the process other than to say that an idea has to be open to any and all criticism. If he thinks there is some way in which the process can be deliberately methodical (in the manner, for example, that we understand scientific inquiry today), he does not say so. Neither does he enter upon any technical epistemological considerations. We shall have occasion to raise questions about various issues in Mill's analysis, but at this point a review of the main points in the chapter is our first priority.

The opening announcement is sorrowfully naive to contemporary ears, for Mill says, "The time, it is to be hoped, is gone by when any defense would be necessary of the 'liberty of the press' as one of the securities against corrupt or tyrannical government." Immediately following, a new point is introduced. "No argument, we may suppose, can now be needed against permitting a legislature or an executive, not identified in interest with the people, to prescribe opinions to them and determine what doctrines or what arguments they shall be allowed to hear." It is startling to hear Mill say "not identified in interest with the people," for his phrase seems to suggest that what amounts to a kind of thought control is only impermissible for a government not identified with the people. The suggestion is soon dispelled, when he says, " . . . I deny the right of the people to exercise such coercion, either by themselves or by their government." The reason is that any silencing of opinion—even that of only one person—inflicts an evil on everyone. "If the opinion is right, they are deprived of the opportunity of exchanging error for truth; if wrong, they lose, what is almost as great a benefit, the clearer perception and livelier impression of truth produced by its collision with error" (*OL*, pp. 15–16).[b]

Mill recognizes that he has made two points. The first is that no one can be certain that the censored opinion is actually false. The sec-

[b]See Appendix A, pp. 84–85.

ond is that it would be an evil to suppress an opinion even if it is known to be false or somehow dangerous. He pursues his first point by claiming that no one is ever entitled to claim infallibility in his or her opinions. Accordingly, no one is ever justified in shutting up someone else on the assumption that he or she already possesses certain truth.

Mill was always sensitive to possible objections to his arguments, and here he anticipates a critical response to what he has said: To silence an opinion need not mean that the authorities are infallible. It might only mean that in their best judgment it is desirable to "prohibit what they think pernicious" (*OL*, p.18).^c Given the choice between prohibiting and not prohibiting, a responsible person has the obligation to choose one or the other and might conscientiously decide for prohibition.

Mill's reply is incisive. One may declare an opinion invalid just so that it will not be examined at all; or one may declare an opinion invalid just because it has been subjected to examination. The censor, in doing the former, is in effect assuming infallibility by refusing to permit a scrutiny of the opinion regarding either its truth or usefulness. It is at this point that Mill makes the remarks quoted at length above. The censor has concluded that he may avoid the social test.[5]

Shortly thereafter Mill reminds us that at one time many persons were convinced that the ideas of Socrates were pernicious, and likewise those of Jesus.[6] He is especially impressed by the fact that the Emperor Marcus Aurelius, one of the most enlightened and noble individuals of the ancient world, saw fit to forbid the observance of Christianity in the Roman Empire. The case of Marcus Aurelius poignantly illustrates how even a person of outstanding character and intellect can make very grave misjudgments—in this case, combating what are perceived to be erroneous or dangerous ideas by forbidding their circulation and persecuting the believers. It is not just wicked people who forbid others the opportunity to judge issues and who affix penalties to certain kinds of belief.

As indicated earlier, there is a second basic argument that Mill submits to us. The first had been of an epistemological nature, arguing that the silencing of an opinion presupposes infallibility. The second introduces moral considerations. Even if we were to know that prevailing opinions are unmistakably true, it would cause grave damage to forbid critical examination of the *grounds* of their truth. The manner in which we entertain an opinion does much to determine

^cSee Appendix A, p. 86.

whether we are descending into passivity or are developing an active intelligence. We can mindlessly accept an opinion as dogma, or we can accept it only because we have engaged in inquiry to determine why it is true. If we adopt the latter procedure, we will exercise and cultivate our intellect; and, because we know for what reasons the conviction is valid, we will be able to uphold and defend it when it is challenged. To use a pertinent example (but not one that Mill himself employed): One could believe in freedom of speech just because some authorities told him to. He would not know any of the considerations that lead to such a conviction. Thus his intellect would remain as dull as ever; and if he were ever in a situation where he had to defend freedom of speech, he would be helpless. In such circumstances, he presumably would not care about defending it, either. Just as Dewey would complain several decades later, Mill objects to religious indoctrination because it weakens rather than strengthens the intellect.

This is not precisely the argument that Mill suggested earlier in the chapter. At the earlier point he had said that it would be wrong to suppress an opinion known to be false; here he says we should never allow received truths to stand unchallenged. These do not amount to quite the same practices, for one could examine received truths without deliberately employing falsehoods. This bit of confusion in Mill's discussion should not obscure the point of this phase of his analysis: Individuals must be free to inquire into and discover the grounds of belief in any judgment. If the judgment is indeed true, it is that much better supported. If it is false, it is now identified as such. Either way, habits of curiosity, inquiry, and verification are exercised and rewarded; and mindless complacency has had no support. If opinions that are certainly false are put to the test, they will be found out, and again the cultivation of intelligent habits has occurred. Mill might well caution us again, moreover, that it would be a mistake just to take it for granted that a proposition is false. Many claims believed with fervent conviction to be true have turned out to be false, and many beliefs widely considered to be false have turned out to be true.

Returning to his concern with the means of discovering truth, Mill observes that in the great majority of controversies we do not find that one of the sides is completely right and the others are completely wrong. Each of the parties probably has merit in at least part of his or her argument. In order to develop and refine the best position that we can, we should, accordingly, encourage open debate between the contending parties, without prejudging the outcome. Mill speaks primarily here about the great controversies of "morals, religion, politics, social relations, and the business of life" (*OL*, p. 35).[d] Although his contention seems obviously sound, we do not find that behavior in the democracies—to say nothing of authoritarian societies—reflects much awareness of it. In the clash of political parties, religious sects, and moral movements, we find each side insisting absolutely on the complete validity of its position, in its entirety. Among some intellectuals, it even seems to pass as a virtue to blast one's adversaries as totally without merit. In our present controversy, for example, between upholders of affirmative action on one side and equal opportunity on the other, the defenders of each position intend to discredit the other completely. With such a stance, none of the partisans can perceive the merit in their opposition. This is not to say that this conflict as it typically exists can be transformed into a unity; but if we were to follow Mill's advice, we would attempt to see what values are really at issue. We have fought for color-blind and gender-blind principles. At the same time, we have found that minorities and women—as well as other groups—have been discriminated against. To follow Mill, we would look for a way to maintain impartial principles while at the same time contriving means to ensure that those who have suffered discrimination are provided remedies that are not themselves prejudicial to others.

Again attending to the formation of our intellectual powers, Mill says, "He who knows only his own side of the case knows little of that. His reasons may be good, and no one may have been able to refute them. But if he is equally unable to refute the reasons on the opposite side, if he does not so much as know what they are, he has no ground for preferring either opinion." The truth, he says, is never "really known but to those who have attended equally and impartially to both sides and endeavored to see the reasons of both in the strongest light" (*OL*, pp. 35, 36).[e] A meritorious, but unusual, practice! Many individuals have taken a passionate stand regarding United States policy toward South Africa. How many of them can give a good account of all sides of the issue? (For that matter, how many can give a full defense of just their own side?)

We have seen that Mill is concerned with the formation and development of the mind. Indeed, before concluding the arguments just summarized, he had digressed to make a point of great consequence. The personal intercourse of submitting opinions to intersubjective scrutiny is vital to the very process of stimulating and developing the

[d]See Appendix A, p. 98.   [e]See Appendix A, pp. 98–99.

intelligence of individual persons. There will always be geniuses, Mill acknowledges, but the intelligence of an entire people can flourish only when it inhabits a medium of uninhibited communication. He speaks forcefully and eloquently on this topic. Here is an excerpt:

> Not that it is solely, or chiefly, to form great thinkers that freedom of thinking is required. On the contrary, it is as much and even more indispensable to enable average human beings to attain the mental stature which they are capable of. There have been, and may again be, great individual thinkers in a general atmosphere of mental slavery. But there never has been, nor ever will be, in that atmosphere an intellectually active people. (*OL*, pp. 32–33)[f]

The individual intelligence will rarely escape from its slumbers, Mill believes, except when it shares in an atmosphere of free thought and discussion.

It is already clear that very high personal demands are made on individuals who would seek a conscientious answer to a question, rather than rest in ignorance and prejudice. Impartiality is required in the pursuit of truth. All sides of a controversy must be given a fair hearing. In this vein the chapter is concluded with a brief but eloquent statement about the behavior proper to the conduct of free inquiry. Mill is disturbed by the proclivity of otherwise decent individuals "to argue sophistically, to suppress facts or arguments, to misstate the elements of the case, or misrepresent the opposite opinion." These are cases where the champion of an idea really does not want you to make up your own mind. He wants to decide for you. Such persons also have a dismaying tendency to engage in "invective, sarcasm, personality, and the like" (*OL*, p. 51).[g] They want to intimidate you or cause you to avoid independent judgment. The most reprehensible behavior of this type, Mill says, is to conduct a discussion by means of personal attack, above all by branding your opponents as morally deficient. Mill recognizes, of course, that all of us are morally deficient in some measure; but attacks on personality are not attacks on an argument. If we were to debate the merits of Nazism with Hitler, we would scrutinize Nazism itself and not hurl curses at Hitler. For his part, be it noted, Mill often engaged in polemic regarding both persons and opinions. This is entirely legitimate. If the subject is the moral character of a particular tyrant, then one must expose what are in fact the qualities of the man. But the in-

[f]See Appendix A, p. 96.   [g]See Appendix A, pp. 107, 108.

quiry into the nature of those traits must always be honest, thorough, impartial.

That summarizes Mill's analysis. There are several questions to be raised about it. As remarked earlier, his essay is not technically elaborated in a manner that would satisfy an epistemologist. We might think that he intends to make much of the claim that every individual is fallible, yet it is not clear what Mill means by the denial of infallibility. He had said, "We can never be sure that the opinion we are endeavoring to stifle is a false opinion"; and he makes a very similar remark in his summary: "[I]f any opinion is compelled to silence, that opinion may, for aught we can certainly know, be true. To deny this is to assume our own infallibility" (*OL*, pp. 16, 50).[h] Taking into account other of Mill's works, however (as well as statements from *On Liberty* itself), the assumption of human fallibility does not mean that we are incapable of achieving certain knowledge. Mill made many confident assertions that we are accumulating certain knowledge at an increasing rate. In the Preface to his *System of Logic*, for example, he refers to the methods by which we have accumulated "laws of the physical world . . . numbered among truths irrevocably acquired and universally assented to . . . " (1872/1956, p. v). In *On Liberty* he tells us, "As mankind improve, the number of doctrines which are no longer disputed or doubted will be constantly on the increase"; and he adds, characteristically, "and the well-being of mankind may almost be measured by the number and gravity of truths which have reached the point of being uncontested" (*OL*, p. 42). Mill believes we are permitted certainty about many matters; so fallibility does not rule out certainty.

His intent in referring to fallibility might well be less epistemological than moral. What fallibility rules out, apparently, is one person or group of persons *deciding for others* what they may and may not believe. He says, "Those who desire to suppress [an opinion] . . . deny its truth; but they are not infallible. *They have no authority to decide the question for all mankind and exclude every other person from the means of judging*" (*OL*, pp. 16–17, emphasis added).[j] A few pages later he makes this clear, saying," . . . I must be permitted to observe that it is not the feeling sure of a doctrine (be it what it may) which I call an assumption of infallibility. It is the undertaking to decide that question *for others*, without allowing them to hear what can be said on the contrary side" (*OL*, p. 22, Mill's emphasis).[k] Mill seems to be

[h]See Appendix A, pp. 85, 107.   [j]See Appendix A, p. 85.
[i]See Appendix A, p. 102.   [k]See Appendix A, p. 90.

making (or confounding) two points. Perhaps a defensible reconstruction consistent with his thinking would hold that there is no certainty without the prior and continuing test of open criticism; and it
would also hold that a conviction of certainty, even if it is warranted,
is never grounds for excluding others from the process of inquiry and
verification.

Insofar as it is a work in theory of knowledge, *On Liberty* is bril-
liantly suggestive, rather than conclusive. Epistemologists might
quarrel with it in many ways. There are still rationalists and intui-
tionists who believe in certainty attained by the individual, unaided
intellect. More conspicuous today among professional philosophers
are those who would contend that Mill's claim to knowledge are too
strong, regardless of how the alleged knowledge is attained.

In the context of our concern with democratic discourse, however, the subtleties of epistemologists are largely irrelevant. It has
been demonstrated in human experience all too often that it is folly to
accept any individual or group as experts simply on their own authority. They will turn out to be our oppressors or manipulators. On the
practical level, we do not believe in infallibility. In democracies, we
do not concede that someone else has the right to do our thinking for
us. We believe in arriving at the grounds of belief rather than blindly
accepting authority. We insist on argument in place of dogma. We
also believe that if certain opinions are systematically protected and
others are systematically shut out, then those behind it are probably
interested in our mindless obedience. Something has been lost both
in the development of intelligence and the attainment of knowledge;
and the opinions that are protected may well be injurious.

In any area of inquiry, when individuals are regarded as authorities, they are accorded that title only because their knowledge has
been achieved and tested according to recognized methods. A distinguished scientist or literary critic has not gained his reputation by
censoring adverse judgments on his work. Mill adumbrates the procedures and norms that have come to be common practice wherever
knowledge and expertise are to be identified, and he warns of the
perils that follow when we become intellectually complacent or dic-
tatorial.

Mill's argument is a greater mixture of moral and epistemological
considerations than he seems to realize. His discussion assumes certain moral ends: the attainment of truth and the freedom to act on
that truth provided the action does no injury to others. As he says
throughout the book, this freedom is the all-important condition of
human progress.

> Where there is a tacit convention that principles are not to be disputed, where the discussion of the greatest questions which can occupy humanity is considered to be closed, we cannot hope to find the generally high scale of mental activity which has made some periods of history so remarkable. (*OL*, p. 33)[l]

> Where not the person's own character but the traditions or customs of other people are the rule of conduct, there is wanting one of the principal ingredients of human happiness, and quite the chief ingredient of individual and social progress. (*OL*, p. 54)

The entire book is about the liberation of the individual, and chapter II is just one phase of the analysis. We have already noticed Mill's contention that freedom is the prime condition of effective intelligence. He had also suggested that the means of "improving mankind" is "free and equal discussion" (*OL*, p. 10). He goes further, concluding, "We have now recognized the necessity to the mental well-being of mankind (on which all other well-being depends) of freedom of opinion, and freedom of the expression of opinion . . ." (*OL*, p. 50).[m]

Mill's accent on freedom is not an endorsement of doing whatever one wants. It excludes doing harm to others, and it requires the performance of (unspecified) social duties. While he is extremely wary of the tyrannies exercised by public opinion, he by no means endorses shutting oneself off from social intercourse. When there is freedom in public discourse, the individual can participate in inquiry and conversation in a manner that will expand his intellectual powers and consequently his powers of action.

If Mill were concerned only with the attainment of truth, his case for freedom would be weaker; for it could very plausibly be argued (in an argument that Mill himself would find difficult to resist) that the process of inquiry would not really be impaired if the least intelligent persons in the community were excluded from it. Mill's reply to this is more in the nature of a moral argument. Presumably, he would invoke his discussion of infallibility, where he claimed on utilitarian grounds that no one should have the authority to decide matters of opinion for others. What reasons can be given for excluding persons from offering opinions and from the opportunity to investigate the reasons for opinions? Why should anyone be excluded from the exchange of ideas and the opportunity for mental development?

In actual social practice we typically find that when individuals and groups are systematically excluded from participation in public discourse, the reason is that the authorities, be they secular or religious, are threatened in their status by the excluded groups. It is a matter of wiping out, or at least detaining, those whom you perceive to be your adversaries; and you are unwilling even to concede to them the possibility that they might have something to offer. (Or perhaps you think they have too much to offer!) To be sure, when there is freedom of speech, many unintelligent things are going to be said; and there will be inflammatory stump speakers, rabble-rousers, liars, hate groups, con artists, cheap politicians, and a further array of propagandists—all of them dressed up in sheep's clothing to exploit this freedom. Yet judgments about who is an exploiter are often difficult to make. One man's vile propagandist is another man's crusading editor. Shall someone be given the authority to decide which is which and thereupon close down the presses? We might attempt to eliminate such exploitation of freedom by establishing a Ministry of Truth, but that would surely be the death of a free society. On the other hand, we could resist the corruptions of discourse by vigorously utilizing our freedom to insist that all significant opinions be subject to the kind of examination that Mill calls for.

Nobody has supposed there should be no limitations on freedom of speech. Mill himself states that

> opinions lose their immunity when the circumstances in which they are expressed are such as to constitute their expression a positive instigation to some mischievous act. An opinion that corn dealers are starvers of the poor, or that private property is robbery, ought to be unmolested when simply circulated through the press, but may justly incur punishment when delivered orally to an excited mob assembled before the house of a corn dealer, or when handed about among the same mob in the form of a placard. (*OL*, p. 53)

We find conscientious disagreement about how limitations on freedom of speech should be determined—as, for example, the history of interpretations of the First Amendment attests. Mill grapples with this problem briefly but not decisively. He does not tell us what he would advocate if a certain view were found pernicious *after* a process of open discussion. He presumably would accept censorship in some form, but with the burden of proof unmistakably on the would-be censors. Although the problem of exceptions to freedom in discourse is serious, its examination is beyond the scope of the present essay.

A fundamental question bearing on Mill's treatment of liberty is whether he regards both scientific and moral questions to be amenable to the same methods of solution. Philosophers throughout history have asked whether the intellectual means of solving moral problems are different in kind from those used in scientific inquiry. It is a question of great import. If science is regarded as the most powerful method of inquiry, or perhaps the exclusive method, then is it possible that the urgent demands of the moral life can be satisfied by an application of science? If not, are there any resources whatever for addressing moral questions? In the text under consideration, Mill wants moral problems above all opened to free public debate. Does he, then, suppose that moral controversies would be resolved by methods or criteria that are the same as those employed in strictly scientific inquiries? On the face of it, one would say yes, since he does not discriminate between science and ethics in this discussion.

From statements in *A System of Logic* and elsewhere, however, it is evident that Mill makes a clear distinction between scientific and evaluative claims.

> Now, the imperative mood is the characteristic of art, as distinguished from science. Whatever speaks in rules or precepts, not in assertions respecting matters of fact, is art; and ethics or morality is properly a portion of . . . art.
> . . . The Method, therefore, of Ethics, can be no other than that of Art, or Practice. . . . (1872/1956, p. 616)

> But though the reasonings which connect the end or purpose of every art with its means belong to the domain of Science, the definition of the end itself belongs exclusively to Art, and forms its peculiar province. (1872/1956, p. 619)

Mill embellishes his point by adding, "A proposition of which the predicate is expressed by the words *ought* or *should be* is generically different from one which is expressed by *is* or *will be*" (1872/1956, pp. 619–20).

Ends are determined by art, and the means to those ends are determined by science. The method and criteria are in each case distinct. In the passage from which the above quotations are taken, Mill states:

> Without attempting in this place to justify my opinion, or even to define the kind of justification which it admits of, I merely declare my conviction, that the general principle to which all the rules of practice ought to conform, and the test by which they should be tried, is that of conduciveness to the happiness of mankind, or rather, of all sentient be-

ings; in other words, that the promotion of happiness is the ultimate principle of Teleology. (1872/1956, p. 621)

He then refers us to his *Utilitarianism* for an analysis and justification
of this principle.

In philosophical scholarship, *Utilitarianism* is notorious for its lack
of both clarity and conclusiveness, and interpreters are still debating
its meaning. Mill repeats Jeremy Bentham's principle of utility: Morally
correct action always aims exclusively at the greatest happiness of the
greatest number of people, where each person counts as one and no
more than one. But unlike Bentham he insists that happiness, or pleasure, must be measured not only quantitatively, but qualitatively. He
says a smaller quantity of high-quality pleasure is to be preferred to a
larger quantity of low-quality pleasure. "It is better to be a human being dissatisfied than a pig satisfied; better to be Socrates dissatisfied
than a fool satisfied" (1863/1957b, p. 14).

The qualitative test raises problems that Mill fails sufficiently to appreciate: The test for determining what is a high-quality pleasure presupposes a moral standard other than utility. When the comparative
quality of two pleasures is in dispute, Mill says, the judgment of those
who have the most experience with both is to be taken as authoritative.
To what criteria do such persons appeal? A sense of dignity, Mill replies
(1863/1957b, p. 13). It is not clear, however, that individuals equally
acquainted with the same pleasures will put them in the same priority; and it might well be that someone with less experience has, in some
sense, better judgment anyway. Then, too, it might be that the sense
of dignity in a Victorian Englishman is unlike that in a late–twentieth-
century American. And why, after all, should the sense of dignity be
morally compelling? Mill does not address these issues. Rather than
being decisive, his test is vague and inconclusive; and it does not lead
to unequivocal policy decisions. (Should we support the interests of
the cultivated and discourage those of a more popular nature?) In addition, Mill offers what he calls a "proof" of the principle of utility
(1863/1957b, ch. IV). This "proof" has convinced almost no one. The
status of Mill's utilitarianism is therefore highly problematic—more so
than he ever imagined. Up to the present day, various reformulations
of utilitarianism have been offered to the philosophic community, and
they have suffered repeated criticisms. Although utilitarianism continues to have gifted defenders, most studies of ethics in the last three
decades have been very harsh with it.[7]

I do not intend that the preceding paragraph should mean that
Mill's utilitarianism is a failure. It is an excellent, if incomplete, account

of the moral life; and, in my judgment, it is superior to the versions that have followed. As noted, utilitarianism has been subjected to responsible criticism, before and after Mill. Much of the criticism, without quite saying so, has been to the effect that the many types of value in moral experience are not reducible to considerations of utility.

Mill's ethical theory would look much better if it were not treated as a version of utilitarianism. When he introduced the qualitative measure of value, Mill was making a heroic attempt to accommodate the varieties of moral experience. The attempt is in evidence in the claim that there are intrinsically higher values. Another significant accommodation lies in Mill's insistence, contrary to Bentham, that self-denial and altruism are humanly possible. Thus a kind of Kantian (and English) devotion to duty is incorporated into Mill's theory. Finally, the fact that his qualitative theory of value does not entail particular moral decisions can also be taken as a great virtue in his ethics. If no one is infallible and if no moral judgment is immune to criticism, then to have open and flexible discussion of moral problems seems the course of wisdom. The result of all these refinements in the views he inherited from Bentham might better be regarded as an eclipse of utilitarianism, as such, rather than its preservation. Such a development would not mean that considerations of utility would be abandoned. It would mean that they would be weighed along with other moral values. Mill did not seem to be aware of how much change he had introduced; and, as remarked earlier, he was unaware of how problematic his own statement of the theory was. But, as I have suggested, it is more problematic *considered as a version of utilitarianism* than if regarded as a distinctive theory in its own right.

These comments are by way of prelude to a return to the question raised earlier: Does Mill think there is a generic difference in the treatment of scientific and moral questions? His explicit statements indicate an affirmative answer, yet this distinction is not introduced in *On Liberty*, where moral and scientific questions are both said to require free and open criticism as the only means for reliable solution. What would be the nature of a moral solution? Would the argument of *On Liberty* mean that the greatest happiness principle is itself to be accepted only provisionally and as open to discussion? Mill does not say so. Early in this chapter I quoted his declaration: "It is proper to state that I forego any advantage which could be derived to my argument from the idea of abstract right as a thing independent of utility. I regard utility as the ultimate appeal on all ethical questions; but it must be utility in the largest sense, grounded on the permanent interests of man as a progressive being" (*OL*, p. 10).[8]

If Mill is assuming infallibility regarding utility, what are the issues that are left open to criticism in moral problems? Inasmuch as we are so often ignorant of the means to our individual and collective good, it is hardly insignificant to say that inquiry and criticism regarding the conditions of the good life are necessary to some achievement of happiness. In reading Mill, however, one is convinced that he means more than this in *On Liberty*. He obviously wants every phase of moral questions to be subject to inquiry and debate. No principle or assumption of any kind is to be immune to criticism and possible revision.

If this is so, then how would moral controversy be resolved? Mill might have believed that scientific inquiries are successfully concluded when all the investigators have the opportunity to propose theories and explanations, contrive and carry out experiments, share the empirical evidence that such ventures yield, and participate in the analysis of the ideas and interpretation of the data. He was sure that one of the decisive elements in determining scientific truth is reference to objective empirical evidence. Are there comparable methods and criteria of moral inquiry? That is, is there some objective and conclusive test for ethical judgments? The preceding analyses suggest that there can be no confident interpretation of Mill on this question.[9]

There are such riches in Mill's ideas that our indecision here is no reason to minimize the significance of this classic essay. It is, remember, a defense of freedom of speech. While Mill is not sufficiently clear about what the nature of methodic communication in either science or ethics might be, he is still clear and convincing about the evils of the imposition of restraints on inquiry and participation. He is equally persuasive regarding the evils of blind acceptance of authority. The recognition of an inherently social test of ideas is new to epistemology; and the notion of such a test is extremely suggestive as an approach to moral controversy.

Mill's discourse is richly innovative. It remains in this chapter to remark wherein his analysis is most innovative of all. Although Mill declares that the social test is necessary for all opinions, including scientific beliefs, he is especially concerned about moral controversies. The resolution of both novel and perennial moral problems is to be taken out of the suffocating closet of private conviction and thrust into the open air of public discussion. Moral quandaries and conflicts are to be addressed by an inherently social process. The convictions of any individual may be submitted to the discourse, and—if Mill is followed—they will be impartially heard. At the same time, nobody's moral opinions are protected from criticism; no one is regarded as infallible. This being so, existing rules of behavior are open to revision, and the solution to moral perplexity might well be to adopt a course of action that is formulated in the process of discourse itself.

This is a radical departure. One of the most abiding traits in the history of moral theory is that moral judgment is reached and certified by the individual as such. It might be an especially wise individual, such as a Platonic philosopher king, who attains to a direct intellectual union with the essential forms of the good and the just. It might be the rational Kantian, who asks *himself* if he can will his maxim to be a universal law. Appearances to the contrary notwithstanding, social-contract theories are no exception to individualism of this sort. The so-called contracts are mythical. They are contrived by some philosopher, who takes the liberty of declaring what would be chosen by rational people in a contract situation, as that philosopher conceives rationality and the nature of the contract situation. This is a case of a self-appointed authority deciding the matter for everyone else.[10] In contrast to all this, Mill is acutely conscious of human fallibility. He is likewise aware of human corrigibility, and he urges that disciplined communication is the means of discovering and correcting our errors. Ethical discourse, accordingly, is fallible; it is also in some sense corrigible; and it might be greatly improved by making it inherently investigative and consultative.

Although Mill's ideas are not worked out, their direction is clear. Unhappily, this dimension of his thought was not pursued by any of his successors in the field of ethics. John Dewey develops the same themes more fully and coherently. Although he expressed great admiration for Mill as a moral philosopher, Dewey's thinking about the social nature of inquiry owes more to Peirce.

Many philosophers have objected to Mill's defense of freedom just because it is predicated on an analysis of the consequences of tyranny and freedom. They believe freedom must be thought of as an inherent right, regardless of its consequences. Philosophizing about rights in this manner is one of the avenues to obscurantism. Nevertheless, it is undeniable that we sometimes attribute rights independently of utility. We might insist in some cases, for example, that a person is entitled to the product of his or her own labor, even if there is a marginally greater utility in distributing it to others. Insofar as a moral philosophy attempts to incorporate the multiple dimensions of moral experience, it cannot reject this form of evaluation out of hand.

Accordingly, an even fuller defense of freedom of speech might be developed along these lines. Such speculations will not be undertaken here, however.

We will return to Mill to present a closely related aspect of his thought, his philosophy of education; but for the present we will examine some of the technicalities of his philosophy of experience. This is a principal source, in Dewey's estimate, of limitations in Mill's grasp of the conditions that might distinguish democracy as an exhibit of human excellence.

CHAPTER 3

Some Defects in Classical Liberalism

Dewey had no real quarrel with anything Mill had said in "Of the Liberty of Thought and Discussion." His objection to Mill, as a late representative of classical liberalism, was that he had failed to identify the conditions essential to *excellence* in public discourse. In his demand for freedom, Mill had succeeded in outlining necessary conditions for excellent communication, but he had erred in assuming them also to be sufficient. Mill's problems are traceable, Dewey believed, to fundamental deficiencies in his philosophy. We can present Dewey's critique by examining two related areas in Mill's thought that Dewey judged to be inadequate: first, philosophy of experience and philosophy of mind; second, philosophical anthropology and philosophy of education.

Mill carried on the assumption of modern philosophy that our experience is constituted of subjective bits and pieces. These are utterly discrete atoms of sensation. They occur, so Mill thought, within the mind. Hence the object of experience is not an external, physical event, but an internal, mental event. These disconnected particles of sensation are united to form complex ideas. The union is not a function of intrinsic relations between objective events; it is created by an exclusively subjective agency, specifically, the laws of the association of ideas. The experience of drinking a cup of coffee, for example, is composed of various sensations. One feels the weight of the cup and its contents and notices its shape, sees the deep brown color of the brew. There is also an aroma from the coffee; then, as one sips, a warm feeling from the drink on the lips and inside the mouth. Finally comes the taste itself, as the drink is savored. According to associationist psychology, all these sensations are united not because they are properties of the coffee in relation to various bodily organs; the weight, shape, color, aroma, temperature, and taste are not properties of the object. They are inherently separate sensations, each one completely subjective, that have been put into a certain combination by the equally subjective associative processes.

These views must make one rather agnostic, at best, about the character and even the existence of what we naively call the external world. Our experience is an impassible barrier between ourselves and this alleged world. When he concentrates on exacting issues in theory of knowledge, Mill himself can allow no more of so-called physical objects in themselves than to call them "permanent possibilities of sensation," and he makes no pretense that he can prove that they have a real existence independent of the mind.[1]

In other moods, however, Mill forgets about the skepticism implied by his technical philosophy. At such moments he judges the habit of mind of dissecting beliefs to be precisely the tool for distinguishing adventitious connections between ideas from real connections between objective phenomena. From his *Autobiography*:

> The very excellence of analysis . . . is that it tends to weaken and undermine whatever is the result of prejudice; that it enables us mentally to separate ideas which have only casually clung together; and no associations whatever could ultimately resist this dissolving force, were it not that we owe to analysis our clearest knowledge of the permanent sequences in nature; the real connexions between Things, not dependent on our will and feelings; natural laws by virtue of which, in many cases, one thing is inseparable from another in fact; which laws, in proportion as they are clearly perceived and imaginatively realized, cause our ideas of things which are always joined together in Nature, to cohere more and more closely in our thoughts. (1873/1957a, p. 89)

He was evidently unaware of how such statements clashed with subjectivism and associationism. His demands in *On Liberty*, of course, are aimed at achieving objective truth. Regardless of such incoherence, Mill remains committed to the philosophy of subjective associations of inherently unrelated sensations. Although he introduced significant changes into associationist psychology, he steadfastly retains its fundamental assumptions.[2] Of the laws of association, he declares in his *System of Logic*, the first is, that similar ideas tend to excite one another. The second is, that when two impressions have been frequently experienced (or even thought of), either simultaneously or in immediate succession, then whenever one of these impressions, or the idea of it, recurs, it tends to excite the idea of the other. The third law is, that greater intensity in either or both of the impressions is equivalent, in rendering them excitable by one another, to a greater frequency of conjunction. These are the laws of ideas, on which I shall not enlarge in this place, but refer the reader to works professedly psychological, in particular to Mr. James Mill's *Analysis of the Phenomena of the Human Mind*, where the principle laws of association, along with many of their applications, are copiously exemplified, and with a masterly hand. (1872/1956, p. 557)

His *System of Logic* is an attempt to interpret all logic, inquiry, and proof as the operation of these processes of association. It is a dismal failure.[3] Indeed, this psychology has been given mortal blows by a number of critics, beginning with T. H. Green in his introduction to Hume's *Philosophical Works* (Green & Grose, 1886/1964) and William James in *The Principles of Psychology* (1890), especially chapters IX and X.

Human motivation is also to be accounted for by associationist psychology. In his edition of the elder Mill's *Analysis*, Mill adds the following comments to his father's theory of motivation:

[I]t is here shewn that a motive to an act consists in the association of pleasure with the act; that a motive to abstain from an act, is the association of pain with it; and we are prepared to admit the truth deduced therefrom, that the one or the other motive will prevail, according as the pleasurable or painful association is the more powerful. What makes the one or the other more powerful, is (conformably to the general laws of association) partly the intensity of the pleasurable or painful ideas in themselves, and partly the frequency of repetition of their past conjunction with the act, either in experience or in thought. In the latter of these two consists the efficacy of education in giving a good or a bad direction to active powers. (Mill, 1869, Vol. 2, p. 262)

Mill does not take this to mean that all behavior is necessarily selfish. He fervently believes in the possibility of altruism, which he urges especially in the second and third chapters of *Utilitarianism*. He thinks that benevolence can be taught by associationist principles. (It is not clear, however, that he can reconcile his remarks about self-sacrifice in *Utilitarianism* with associationist doctrine.) Notice in this above quotation that Mill believes a good moral education to consist in the frequent repetition of associations. He does not say that pleasure and pain are causes of association. Rather, ideas associated with pleasure and pain occur according to the laws of association. Notice finally that he does not speak of an action *being* painful, but says pain is *associated* with it.

Like T. H. Green and William James, Dewey was a trenchant critic of this philosophy of experience. He focused particularly on the following: The empiricists, Mill included, viewed mind as wholly passive. It is sprayed with intrinsically unrelated sensations from without, and the alleged laws of mental association amalgamate these atomic experiences into complex ideas. Ideas, according to this theory, are summaries or composites of antecedently given (and unrelated) sense data. They are mirrors of the antecedently given, if of anything at all.

Dewey, on the other hand, characterizes experience in terms of activity; and mind and thinking are derivative of activity. To take the passive beholding of sensations as the model of experience is to ignore the fact that our intercourse with the world is one of active behavior with it. We come at objects and take hold of them, and manipulate them for use and enjoyment—as the child grasps a shiny toy and experiments with it. Experience is a matter of "doing and undergoing," as Dewey says, speaking in a vocabulary distinctly different from Mill's.

> Wherever there is life, there is behavior, activity. In order that life may persist, this activity has to be both continuous and adapted to the environment. This adaptive adjustment, moreover, is not wholly passive; is not a mere matter of the moulding of the organism by the environment. . . . In the interests of the maintenance of life there is transformation of some elements in the surrounding medium. The higher the form of life, the more important is the active reconstruction of the medium. . . . The civilized man goes to distant mountains and dams streams. He builds reservoirs, digs channels, and conducts the waters to what had been a desert. He searches the world to find plants and animals that will thrive. He takes native plants and by selection and cross-fertilization improves them. He introduces machinery to till the soil and care for the harvest. . . .
>
> Such transformation scenes are so familiar that we overlook their meaning. We forget that the inherent power of life is illustrated in them. Note what a change this point of view entails in the traditional notions of experience. Experience becomes an affair primarily of doing. The organism does not stand about, Micawberlike, waiting for something to turn up. It does not wait passive and inert for something to impress itself upon it from without. The organism acts in accordance with its own

structure, simple or complex, upon its surroundings. As a consequence the changes produced in the environment react upon the organism and its activities. The living creature undergoes, suffers, the consequences of its own behavior. This close connection between doing and suffering or undergoing forms what we call experience. (Dewey, 1920, pp. 128–29)

Experience is an activity of the organism and the environment together as an inclusive process, in which the live creature struggles to function with its surroundings, constituted of a myriad of processes tending to uncertain outcomes. This highly dynamic context is in sharp contrast to the view of the empiricists, who postulated mind as a photosensitive receptacle, as it were, quiescently receiving sensations, which are automatically bound into ideas.

> So far as anything beyond a bare present is recognized by the established doctrine, the past exclusively counts. Registration of what has taken place, reference to precedent, is believed to be the essence of experience. Empiricism is conceived of as tied up to what has been, or is, "given." But experience in its vital form is experimental, an effort to change the given; it is characterized by projection, by reaching forward into the unknown; connection with a future is its salient trait. . . . An experience that is an undergoing of an environment and a striving for its control in new directions is pregnant with connections. (Dewey, 1917, p. 6)[4]

The central concept in Dewey's analysis of human nature is habit, which he develops very suggestively in *Human Nature and Conduct*. All behavior is the functioning of habit. The fundamental notion in Dewey's idea of habit is that it is an activity of the biological organism *and* the environment. Both terms in the relation—organism and environment—are constitutive of human nature and behavior. The defining characteristics of human nature are not, then, an exclusive possession of the organism. Neither are they a form pressed from without on passive clay. The organism possesses an indefinite plurality of native impulses, but these are not in themselves, Dewey argues, forms of action; they are not serviceable powers. An impulse only becomes a definite mode of conduct as a consequence of interaction with the environment; and it is the specific nature of the environment that determines just what that mode will be. Everyone has the impulse to seek food, for example, but the specific forms of food seeking are indefinitely plural. Hence there are hunters, gatherers, farmers of all kinds, fishermen, persons who go to the supermarket, or to fast-food outlets, or to restaurants; there are gourmet cooks and those who just eat frozen dinners. The farmer has definite forms of behavior to till the soil. These forms are not innate in the farmer. They depend upon the nature of the necessary interactions. The activity of hoeing, for example, depends on the simple facts of the physical constitution of the soil, the physical constitution of the human oganism, the need to remove weeds from the cultivated area, and the physical properties requisite in the tool to function in this situation. The habit of hoeing is a function of all these conditions.

Dewey's concept of habit might be clarified by likening habits to tools or other instruments, such as the hoe. The development of hoes and rakes, plows and harvesters, depends on the needs of the farmer, his physiological formation, and the conditions with which he must work. Thus the hoe, and any implement or machine, constitutes a harmonious adjustment of man and nature, where the nature of the adjustment depends as much upon man as upon nature. According to Dewey's analysis, our habits are like that hoe.

The single most important factor in the formation of habit is the social environment. As other human beings respond to us, make demands upon us, help, hinder, or support us in various ways, we develop particular habits of conduct. These interactions determine our distinctive interests and talents, our virtues and vices as well. "Honesty, chastity, malice, peevishness, courage, triviality, industry, irresponsibility are not private possessions of a person. They are working adaptations of personal capacities with environing forces" (Dewey, 1922b, p. 16). As an individual matures, his or her habits become more plentiful, complex, and fixed. Accordingly, as we grow up, our particular personality is increasingly determinative of the nature of the interactions in which we engage. Should an agent have a strong and distinctive character, variations in the environment would less and less have a decisive role in behavior. For this reason (among others) early education is extremely important to Dewey.

Although the theory sketched in *Human Nature and Conduct* is remarkably consistent and suggestive, it was more in the way of a new beginning than a finality in our thinking about human nature. If Dewey's basic point of view is accepted, there is still much in the way of refinement and qualification that would be required. Even so, there is something radical in his position. The radical character of the idea of habit consists in the notion that it is a relation that cuts across the merely physical distinction between the individual and his surroundings. The inclusive processes of organism/environment determine what our particular nature will be; and it is likewise this inclusive process that determines behavior. If Dewey's notion of habit has validity, it wipes out in one stroke the Cartesian dualism that has dominated modern philosophy. That is, man is not a separate substance with inherent essence or laws that determine his behavior. The processes of growth, development, and character formation must be thought of primarily as functions of social relations. Then it becomes possible to investigate how human personality varies with variations in the environment. With the acquisition of such knowledge, education might become truly effectual.

The process of determination of habit is at the same time the determination of experience. In accordance with the notion that experience is a function of organism and environment together, Dewey insists that experience is not something going on within someone's mind. ''It is not experience which is experienced, but nature—stones, plants, animals, disease, health, temperature, electricity, and so on'' (1925a, p. 12). The properties of an object are not inherent in its supposed essence or substance. Neither are they subjective inventions. Rather, they are properties of the conjoint activities of many processes. This would be as true of the mass and shape of the cup of coffee as of its color, aroma, taste, and temperature. All are objective properties, depending for their existence in a given situation on a particular combination of circumstances. The existence of many qualities, such as heat and color, requires the activity of a sentient organism. To say that sense organs are among the necessary conditions of the existence of various properties is not to say that the properties are therefore within those organs or within the mind. Certain processes are necessary conditions of *any* property—of the dimensions of Saturn, for example; but that does not mean that the dimensions of Saturn disappear into those processes.

The objects of experience, then, are the events and properties of the real world; and they do not come to us in isolated bits and pieces. We experience events in their relations, rather than concoct them out of isolated sensations. Principally due to activity, we learn that the relations between the different events of experience are contingent upon definite processes: The harvest is ruined due to premature frost, the salt causes the wound to sting, the kind words bring gratitude and trust. Any event in experience becomes significant of specific functions of nature. Experience becomes increasingly meaningful. Our morning cup of coffee is not really an assembly of sensations. Coffee means something made from beans, purchased from the store, prepared in a certain way; something that tastes good and wakes you up; something delightfully shared with your friends or spouse. Thus experience grows and becomes enriched with meaning and resources.

Dewey's philosophy restores the continuity of experience and nature that had been radically breached in modern thought. In the normal course of experience, events gain in meaning and we learn what to do with natural events in order to achieve definite ends. According to Dewey's concept of nature, the perils, pains, loves, delights, and tragedies of mortal existence are one and all functions of natural processes. It is in principle possible to determine the conditions of both the welcome and unwelcome outcomes so that we might contrive means for avoiding the latter and attaining the former.

The import of this analysis is crucial: According to Dewey, we are in intimate, if not always pleasant, union with nature; while for Mill nature remains an unintelligible cipher. From Mill's basic assumptions, the events of experience have no significance regarding the real relationships in the world upon which life and welfare depend. If Mill's philosophy of experience were consistently followed, we would have no clue as to how we could deliberately identify and pursue the precious events that natural processes afford. His philosophy of experience is a recipe for impotence.

Mill, of course, believed in taking an active and energetic role in shaping events of experience for human welfare. However, he could not do so in terms of his own philosophy, but only in spite of it. He had a peculiarly incoherent world view, and he was therefore unable to explore all the potentialities that experience affords for intelligent conduct. Consider again the empiricists' conception of ideas.

The orthodox empiricist believed that an idea is a summary of antecedently given sensations. It is a record of what has already happened. Against this view, Dewey identifies ideas as instruments of action. Their meaning refers not to the past, but the future. Following Peirce and James in the biological point of view, he holds that an idea is an anticipation of the outcome of present contingencies. It is a means by which an agent adjusts his behavior with his environment to conduct natural processes to a desirable outcome.

Consideration of the nature of meanings will help to clarify Dewey's position. The meanings of events are relations. For an individual event, its meaning is the very relationships that bring it into being, change it, and that it exerts on other events in conjunction with other processes. The meaning of steel, then, consists of the variations it undergoes in its relations to such other things as mining and smelting, heating and cooling, mixing with other metals, molding into various shapes, withstanding various stresses, being used for a plurality of purposes, and so forth.

According to this theory of meaning, any statement about the nature of something has reference to the outcome of deliberately introduced changes, or to changes that occur in the natural course of events. Meanings are stated as the changes that will come about when prescribed operations are carried out on specific conditions. In talking of steel, for example, we say things of the following sort: ''If we heat this material to so many degrees, it will become molten.'' ''At such and such a temperature it will be malleable and will have certain structural properties.'' ''If this is steel, it can be used to build houses, automobiles, and bridges.'' In every instance, there is a behavior prescribed in order to bring about a subsequent result.

In having ideas, we possess the meaning of events. We know the nature of something insofar as we can function with it in predictable ways. For an individual to have the idea of, again, steel, is for him to be prepared to act with that metal in such a way that he can bring about predictable results with it. Hence an engineer or an architect has a richer meaning of steel than a philosophy professor. He knows much more about how to function with steel for definite outcomes in a variety of contexts.

To have an idea is neither to have an image or a cluster of sensations nor to possess a Platonic form. It is to be explicitly prepared to act with the event denoted. Neither Plato's essentialism nor Mill's sensationalism provides this efficacy, whether we are talking about steel, coffee, language, or education. A Platonic Idea gives us no information about how variations in processes of change can be introduced in order to regulate further change; and neither does Mill's cluster of sensations. (Indeed, as noted above, Mill's theory of ideas fails to establish *any* link between experience and nature—even to past events.)

The focal point in the pragmatic analysis is that ideas give us power over events. With true ideas, we have one of the necessary conditions for the prediction and control of natural processes. This conception, unavailable to the associationists, is of great consequence to Dewey, who is forever saying we should guide our conduct with ideas. By this he does *not* mean that we should conform to the antecedently given. He vigorously opposes such conformity; he has something more creative in mind. Utilizing his technical analysis of meaning, he intends that we should use ideas as instruments for managing present conditions to bring about a reconstruction of problematic circumstances. Rather than use ideas simply as precedents to follow, we can use them for intelligent innovation. A creative hypothesis will specify actions to be taken in a definite situation in order to transform it into a new condition.

Pragmatism . . . does not insist upon antecedent phenomena but upon consequent phenomena; not upon the precedents but upon the possibilities of action. And this change in point of view is almost revolutionary in its consequences. An empiricism which is content with repeating facts already past has no place for possibility and for liberty. It cannot find room for general conceptions or ideas, at least no more than to consider them as summaries or records. But when we take the point of view of pragmatism we see that general ideas have a very different role to play than that of reporting and registering past experiences. They are bases for organizing future observations and experiences. (Dewey, 1925b, p. 12)[5]

With the vague term 'idea', Dewey typically means a definite hypothesis, a plan of action that specifies actions to be taken with our surroundings in order to attain a particular result. A hypothesis, framed in the conditional mode, prescribes certain operations to be undertaken, and it predicts that if the operations are carried out as directed, a certain result will follow. This is what an experimental hypothesis in the sciences does. A scientific hypothesis might prescribe, for example, that a carefully defined program of diet and exercise will reduce the incidence of heart disease by a certain percentage in a given population. If the practice is carried out as directed, the hypothesis is thereby tested for its validity.

Hypotheses as Dewey understands them are not just guesses about what might be the cause of a given phenomenon (although they often are just that). More than this, they are proposals for the deliberate revision and management of ongoing processes in order to wrest from nature what can never be attained by mere observation. Following the prescription of his hypothesis, the scientist deliberately introduces some novel reconstruction of natural events. If this reconstruction brings about the predicted result, the hypothesis is insofar verified. Progress in science, Dewey believes, has been largely a product of the introduction of innovative hypotheses, which are subject to test and revision by the community of inquirers.

He looks for progress in human affairs by adopting the same technique. Whenever we are faced with some kind of obstacle or perplexity, we should consider a means of reconstructing the situation in order to bring about a more satisfactory state of affairs. Our plan of action would dictate specified interventions in order to produce a desired result. If, for example, our problematic situation is that elementary school students are bored, passive, dull, and unimaginative, then we conceive a plan for the reform of the educational process that will make them eager, active, bright, and inventive. When we institute changes according to the plan, we are directing our conduct by ideas; and if the plan has the predicted result, the idea is at least provisionally warranted.

Dewey stresses the creative dimension of this process. The thinker or thinkers conceive of new ways of challenging their problematic situations, and they propose to introduce hitherto unexampled relationships between events—new ways of teaching, for example. On the other hand, if we just meet our problems in the old ways, we shall do no more than repeat our past mistakes; and we shall make no headway in succeeding where we have characteristically failed. Given the continued obduracy of human problems and their growing complexity, Dewey had high hopes for a truly experimental approach to our common predicaments.

John Stuart Mill was as admiring of creativity as Dewey. We find repeated praise in Mill for bold and innovative speculation, for creative genius. Indeed, as we saw in the preceding chapter, he regards courageous and intelligent originality as the principal engine of human progress. The problem with Mill's position, again, is that his theory of the nature of ideas permits him no systematic understanding of how these traits can be incorporated into disciplined inquiry. This is evident in his philosophy of scientific method, where there is insufficient recognition of the role of creative hypotheses. In his explicit discussion of the methods of inquiry, there is no mention at all of hypotheses.[6] He does refer to them elsewhere, but in that instance he does not see them as instruments in a process that is at once inventive, rigorous, and experimental. They are not instruments for the deliberate and creative reconstruction of problematic conditions.

In Dewey's terms, Mill's theory of experience prohibited him from formulating any effective notion of creative intelligence. The British liberals (including Mill) "did not recognize the place in experiment of comprehensive social ideas as working hypotheses in direction of action." They failed to realize that "experimental method in science demands a control by comprehensive ideas, projected in possibilities to be realized in action" (1935/1963b, pp. 42–43).[n] Analyses like Mill's identified instruments that would be effective in the criticism of existing ideas, but they lacked the understanding required for the constructive use of organizing hypotheses. Dewey writes, "The instruments of analysis, of criticism, of dissolution, that were employed were effective for the work of release. But when it came to the problem of organizing the new forces and the new in-

[n]See Appendix B, p. 124.

dividuals whose modes of life they radically altered into a coherent social organization, possessed of intellectual and moral directive power, liberalism was well-nigh impotent" (1935/1963b, p. 53).°

Mill and his cohorts were very good at taking ideas apart, but they lacked the philosophic wherewithal to conceive ideas as instruments for the deliberate redirection of events. With the limitations imposed by his philosophy, Mill could do no better than formulate a model of discourse consisting just of criticism. Creative, reconstructive discourse could not be conceived in his terms.

Just as Dewey's liberal predecessors had pulverized experience into smithereens, they reduced society to nothing more than an aggregate of individuals complete in themselves apart from their social relations. Dewey believed that both this philosophy of mind and of society were politically motivated. Mill and the liberals were critical of the old order. The abuses of this order had been defended largely by claiming that the status quo represented an inherent structure of reality; but the inherent structure was a myth—nothing more than a persistence of what had been established in history. "In every case, active reformers were 'empiricists' in the philosophical sense. They made it their business to show that some current belief or institution that claimed the sanction of innate ideas or necessary conceptions, or an origin in an authoritative revelation of reason, had in fact proceeded from a lowly origin in experience, and had been confirmed by accident, by class interest or by biased authority" (Dewey, 1920, pp. 126–27). The social order was uncritically dominated by the past. In addition to reducing all ideas to sensations, the liberals could attack this dominance by assuming that being has no inherent structure, but is simply a collection of entities, each of which is self-complete. Dewey summarizes:

> Grateful recognition is due early liberals for their valiant battle in behalf of freedom of thought, conscience, expression and communication. The civil liberties we possess, however precariously today, are in large measure the fruit of their efforts and those of the French liberals who engaged in the same battle. But their basic theory as to the nature of intelligence is such as to offer no sure foundation for the permanent victory of the cause they espoused. They resolved mind into a complex of external associations among atomic elements, just as they resolved society itself into a similar compound of external associations among individuals, each of whom had his own independently fixed nature. . . . Mill's own contention that psychological laws of the kind he laid down

°See Appendix B, p. 127.

were prior to the laws of men living and communicating together, acting and reacting upon one another, was itself a political instrument forged in the interest of criticism of beliefs and institutions that he believed should be displaced. The doctrine was potent in exposure of abuses; it was weak for constructive purposes. . . . The theory of mind held by the early liberals advanced beyond dependence on the past but it did not arrive at the idea of experimental and constructive intelligence. (1935/1963b, pp. 42–43)[p]

Much as Mill demanded excellence in public discourse, he was unable to incorporate into his analyses the instruments that would make such discourse at the same time creative and experimental. This is the first general objection to Mill's philosophy from Dewey's point of view.

The second general objection is that Mill's philosophy precludes an understanding of how intellectual and moral habits are generated. Mill recognized as much as Dewey that we can never attain distinction in our public converse unless the participants are equipped with the right moral and intellectual virtues; but Dewey was convinced that Mill's philosophy of education was so deficient as to be helpless.

Again, from Mill's point of view, we have the passive reception of sensations, which are then bound into more elaborate patterns, depending on their order, frequency, and intensity. With sufficient frequency of repetition, the person will form ever-stronger associations of pain with certain kinds of action and pleasure with others. According to this psychology, for example, one would learn to be rational when the logical relations between ideas are indurated by association. One would *want* to be rational when there is a frequent association between rationality and pleasure. Likewise, we may receive ideas in such a manner that we associate our pleasures and pains with those of others, and in this way we become moral. The learning process appears to depend largely on the order in which sensations are given to us.

Mill's own upbringing was an exact specimen of education according to associationism, conducted personally and exclusively by the most devout of associationists, James Mill. In his *Autobiography*, the younger Mill essentially endorses the solitary, intellectualized education he received from his father. There the two of them sat at the table in James Mill's room, going over John's lessons. The father gave the son daily assignments, beginning at the age of three with the

[p]See Appendix B, p. 124.

study of classical Greek language and literature. This subject was followed by a torrent of others, in great volume. The son would daily report on his results and answer questions about the subject matter. Most of the day was taken up in this way. John would have questions of his own. It was one of the father's methods to refrain as much as possible from answering them, insisting that the boy figure them out for himself. (It is not clear how this phase of the process was associationist. It seems to call upon native powers independent of association.)

The process continued until Mill was fourteen. This prodigiously precocious boy digested a massive body of knowledge and mastered the prevailing tools of inquiry and criticism. He did so uncomplainingly, yet the environment was terribly serious, even cheerless; and it was not affectionate. The *Autobiography* states that James gave very little praise or encouragement to John. He was much more concerned to impress on him that he was not doing very well. Hence Mill states, in praising this pedagogy,

> If I had been by nature extremely quick of apprehension, or had possessed a very accurate and retentive memory, or were of a remarkably active and energetic character, the trial would not be conclusive; but in all these natural gifts I am rather below than above par; what I could do, could assuredly be done by any boy or girl of average capacity and healthy physical constitution: and if I have accomplished anything, I owe it, among other fortunate circumstances, to the fact that through the early training bestowed on me by my father, I started, I may fairly say, with an advantage of a quarter of a century over my contemporaries. (1873/1957a, p. 19)

The only serious fault in this education, as the younger Mill regarded it, was that there was little or no attention to the cultivation of feeling or sentiment. James Mill was contemptuous of such things; so his son was trained only to think and to act, not to luxuriate in the qualitative world of feeling. When John Stuart suffered an acute depression in his twentieth year, lasting to about his twenty-fourth, one of the incidents that rescued him, he says, was the discovery that he still had feelings—in this instance for a family depicted in a personal memoir. He then set about to cultivate his feelings, mainly through reading romatic poets, Wordsworth above all; he also enjoyed Carlyle and Coleridge, without accepting their philosophies.

In the following chapter a more thorough look will be taken at Mill's philosophy of education. We have seen that he thought of himself as largely endorsing the educational theory of associationist psychology. We know that Dewey was a severe critic of associationism, and his judgment of it is predictable. Here he refers to it as sensationalism. The following quotation omits the second of Dewey's three criticisms.

> There are at least three serious defects of sensationalistic empiricism as an educational philosophy of knowledge. (*a*) The historical value of the theory was critical; it was a dissolvent of current beliefs about the world and political institutions. It was a destructive organ of criticism of hard and fast dogmas. But the work of education is constructive, not critical. It assumes not old beliefs to be eliminated and revised, but the need of building up new experience into intellectual habitudes as correct as possible from the start. Sensationalism is highly unfitted for this constructive task.
>
> . . . (*c*) A thoroughly false psychology of mental development underlay sensationalistic empiricism. Experience is in truth a matter of *activities*, instinctive and impulsive, in their interactions with things. What even an infant 'experiences' is not a passively received quality impressed by an object, but the effect which some activity of handling, throwing, pounding, tearing, etc., has upon an object, and the consequent effect of the object upon the direction of activities. . . . Fundamentally, . . . the ancient notion of experience as a practical matter is truer to fact than the modern notion of it as a mode of knowing by means of sensations. The neglect of the deep-seated active and motor factors of experience is a fatal defect of the traditional empirical philosophy. (1916, pp. 278–80)

Consistently with his philosophy of experience and his notion of habit, Dewey's philosophy of education stresses the centrality of activity in learning. This is not mindless or otherwise undirected activity, however. Much of education, Dewey held, should be devoted to the process of inquiry, of discovery. This is not only because one learns better what he finds out for himself than what he is told to remember. It is also because learning the methods of inquiry ought to be a higher priority than simply trying to retain the results of someone else's inquiry (or someone else's authority). Finally, it is because the process of experimental inquiry is the paradigm of the union of theory and practice: The process of intelligent inquiry always requires the formulation of a hypothesis. The hypothesis, as we noted earlier, is a proposal for resolving the problematic situation of inquiry. That is, the hypothesis specifies a certain course of activity in the form of an experiment. If we reconstruct our present situation according to prescription, then (it is predicted) we will attain our hoped-for result. That is, we will find out whether the conditions spelled out in the hypothesis are causally related to the predicted phenomenon. The problematic situation might be specifically scientific, like the search for a cure for cancer; but it could also be an individual problem, such as trying to find a job: If I prepare myself in the appropriate ways and demonstrate reliability and energy, I am apt to be hired by this company. It could be a matter of public policy, such as looking for an answer to the problem of disposing of toxic wastes. Dewey believed the best education is one in which the students pursue the process of inquiry from its problematic stage through experimentation, test, and revision.

While Mill had basic insight into the social dimension of criticism and verification in *On Liberty,* he does not there or elsewhere develop the insight or its implications.[7] Dewey, on the other hand, seizes the idea of the social nature of inquiry. He tirelessy reminds his readers that in contemporary science the only acceptable methods of inquiry and verification are social. A plurality of inquirers attack a given problem, formulating various hypotheses and conducting various experiments. They communicate with each other face to face and by means of publication. In this manner they create, test, revise, and refine. No scientific result is veridical unless it is a product of this process. Knowledge, then, is a product only of a community of inquirers.

In order to incorporate social method into the learning process, Dewey would have students function as a community of inquirers. The principal reason for doing so, however, is not to make them good scientists. It is to make them good citizens. Just as individualism will not succeed in solving scientific problems, neither will it succeed in solving moral problems. That is, Dewey was convinced, we must engage in a process of intelligent cooperation if we are to be successful in addressing our morally problematic situations. The individual intellect cannot attain to scientific truth, and it cannot solve problems of moral conflict and disagreement.[8]

There will be an elaboration of social intelligence in chapter 5. My concern at the moment is to emphasize that education in many of its phases must proceed as an explicitly social process, involving shared thinking and shared activity. In the school (and elsewhere, one hopes) students acquire habits of conduct such that common enterprises are conceived and carried out. Each participant is aware of his or her own role in relation to others as part of the whole. Each person knows what the others are doing in the interactive process. This requires communication and the development of such virtues as cooperativeness and open-mindedness. The result of such learning is mastery of the practices of democratic social control, in contradistinction to control by authority, by command and obedience. "*Mind* as a concrete thing is precisely the power to understand things in terms of the use made of them; a socialized mind is the power to understand them in terms of the use to which they are turned in joint or shared situations. *And mind in this sense is the method of social control''* (Dewey, 1916, p. 38).

As the preceding remarks suggest, an individual needs more than simply intellectual skills to participate in democratic discourse. He or she must have certain moral qualities as well. These are acquired in practice. Whether they be virtues or vices, they are habits; and they are derivative of social interaction. The principal way that one becomes a moral person is not through formal instruction, as associationist psychology would have it. Rather, as one participates in social conduct, he is rewarded or punished for the actions he performs. We learn the meaning of our actions as social functions or dysfunctions. Dewey does not think of these rewards and punishments as extrinsic to behavior. When an individual shares with others in inherently satisfying activity, the satisfaction is quite literally a function of that participation; likewise when one engages in unpleasant or hurtful activity with others. All social practices are therefore educative. A society may function in such a way that its institutions tend to produce, say, democratic persons, or it may be such that it produces persons who seek and obey authority.

Dewey, as we have seen, found the associationist view grossly inadequate as a philosophy of education. Hence Mill would be subject to his critique. Interestingly, however, this is not how Dewey responds to Mill specifically. His objection is that Mill postulates a self-complete individual prior to social interaction. Mill assumes that human nature is prior to activity. Dewey more than once rebukes Mill for his statement in *A System of Logic:*

> The laws of the phenomena of society are, and can be, nothing but the laws of the actions and passions of human beings united together in the social state. Men, however, in a state of society, are still men; their actions and passions are obedient to the laws of individual human nature. Men are not, when brought together, converted into another kind of substance, with different properties; . . . . Human beings in society have no properties but those which are derived from, and may be resolved into, the laws of the nature of individual man. (Mill, 1872/1956, p. 573)

Statements like that got Dewey's hackles up. They sound like runaway individualism; and they evidently deny much that Dewey believed, namely, that human nature is formed through interaction.

Dewey, however, fails to identify the real nature of Mill's individualism. The import of the quotation above is really innocuous from Dewey's point of view. The explicit individualism that Mill acknowledges consists just of the laws of the association of ideas, which are the fixed and innate possession of each individual. This assumption in fact proclaims the omnipotence of culture. With knowledge of these laws, educators can feed individuals with ideas in a certain sequence and thereby form their intellectual and moral character in any way they wish. Mill expressly declares as much: "It is certain that, in human beings at least, differences in education and in outward circumstances are capable of affording an adequate explanation of by far the greatest portion of character, and that the remainder may be in great part accounted for by physical differences in the sensations produced in individuals by the same external or internal cause," rather than by innate features of human nature (1872/1956, p. 561). Mill goes on to acknowledge the presence of instincts, but he adds that "these instincts may be modified to any extent, or entirely conquered, in human beings, . . . by other mental influences, and by education" (1872/1956, p. 561). *The Utility of Religion* declares: "The power of education is almost boundless; there is not one natural inclination which it is not strong enough to coerce and, if needful, to destroy by disuse" (Mill, 1874/1958a, p. 53).

In *Nature*, which is a critique of the natural law approach to ethics, Mill again claims the virtual omnipotence of education, saying, "only after a long course of artificial education did good sentiments become so habitual, and so predominant over bad, as to arise unprompted when occasion called for them. . . . The truth is that there is hardly a single point of excellence belonging to human character which is not decidedly repugnant to the untutored feelings of human nature" (1874/1958a, p. 32).

Dewey's objections to Mill seem to be wide of the mark. Indeed, given Mill's statements above, Dewey should seem rather to object to the passivity and shapelessness of the human subject, which is typical of his critique of associationism. Yet there is a sense in which Mill *is* worthy of being examined for his individualism from a Deweyan perspective. This is an examination Dewey himself never undertook. This is the sort of individualism that goes back at least to John Locke. It was given expression by Mill in many ways, yet Mill was not aware of it. The fact is that Mill, without realizing it, entertained two conceptions of human nature; and hence he was committed to two distinctly different philosophies of education.

CHAPTER 4

Mill's Philosophies of Education

We have seen that Mill was a committed associationist, and he was therefore committed to the potency of culture in determining the qualities of human nature. At other times, however, he takes quite a different view. He spontaneously thinks in terms of innate faculties, conceived as ready-made powers of thought and action. This is a conception of human nature as active, self-contained, and requiring for its development only the opportunity to flourish under its own powers. In this context, education consists primarily of the cultivation of the faculties through use and exercise. The proper environment for this sort of education is freedom; that is, the absence of restraint upon the individual to exercise his or her native powers until they become fully actual. This is an anthropology and pedagogy very close to that of his philosophic forebear, John Locke. Locke's philosophy is the classic expression of British individualism, and the spirit of Locke and the English tradition penetrate deeply into Mill. Since Mill was unaware that he repeatedly gave expression to this view, he provides no systematic account of it. For that we must look to Locke himself.

In *An Essay Concerning Human Understanding*, Locke understands human nature largely in terms of innate faculties. "And such [operations of the soul] are *perception, thinking, doubting, believing, reasoning, knowing, willing,* and all the different actings of our own minds" (1700/1958, Vol. 1, p. 123). We have inherent powers of remembering, reasoning, willing, judging, imagining, and the like. Thus there are innate powers to perform the characteristic functions of human nature. If you want an explanation of how it is, say, that we remember, the answer is that it is due to our faculty of memory. (Locke did not understand that such an answer is completely unhelpful.)

The faculties are original. They are neither created nor shaped by converse with the world. One is not born with them full-blown, however. Locke says their maturation is due to "use and exercise." In his little volume, *Of the Conduct of the Understanding*, he writes, "We are born with faculties and powers capable almost of anything, such at least as would carry us further than can easily be imagined; but it is only the exercise of those powers which gives us ability and skill in anything that leads us towards perfection" (1706/1966, pp. 41–42). The process can be likened to the manner in which we develop our muscles: Do so many sit-ups and push-ups to begin with. Each day increase the number of repetitions and eventually one will have well-developed abdomen, arms, and shoulders. Locke himself uses a similar comparison, concluding "As it is in the body, so it is in the mind; practice makes it what it is, and most even of those excellences which are looked on as natural endowments will be found, when examined into more narrowly, to be the product of exercise and to be raised to that pitch only by repeated actions" (1706/1966, p. 42). He elsewhere characterizes the responsibilities of the educator as primarily those of protecting the student from inhibiting influences. "The studies which he sets him on are but, as it were, the exercises of his faculties and employment of his time, to keep him from sauntering and idleness, to teach him application and accustom him to take pains, and to give him some little taste of what his own industry must perfect" (1693/1968, p. 198).[1] The faculties of the student require only that they not be impeded. This is rather like taking care of a garden: If we keep it clear of pests and weeds, it will grow to maturity on its own. Locke's conception of education is in stark contrast to that of the associationists, who monitor every step of the process to see to it that ideas are given in a sequence that will ensure their continued association.[2]

Locke's view of human nature is conspicuous in his extremely influential *Second Treatise of Government* (1690/1960), which makes much of the alleged social contract. Locke conceives of man in a state of nature as being in full possession of his faculties. He is a fully rational and moral being prior to entering into the contract and the subsequent social relationships.[3] That is, Locke believes that the individual becomes autonomous, civilized, and self-sufficient without the benefit of a social order. In the presocial condition, as Locke conceives it, man is invested with rights, principally those of life, liberty, and estate. Locke's conception of individual rights is largely indebted to his conception of human nature. If the individual is self-sufficient and virtuous in his original state, then he neither needs nor wants social assistance. He only requires to be left alone to pursue his own good in his own way. He needs only freedom. Without the constraints that might be imposed by arbitrary authority, he will flourish on his own.

In philosophic literature a distinction is made between negative and positive freedom. 'Negative freedom' denotes a condition in which there is no restraint. 'Positive freedom' refers to a condition in which agents possess effective powers of conduct. Negative freedom as an exclusive political ideal is often criticized on the grounds that individuals are not empowered to act only in that no one is restraining them. Effective powers of action, the critics say, have to be conferred upon the individual by a deliberately educative process. If individuals are to be positively liberated, there must be social institutions devoted to the nurture and development of human nature. In terms of this distinction between negative and positive freedom, Locke's philosophy is paradigmatic of negative freedom.

When Mill is read with Locke's views in mind, the presence of Locke's ideas is found on page after page. Such expressions as "active exercise of the faculties," "spontaneous self-development," "unfolding of the inward forces," "cultivation of human nature," and the like are found by the score in Mill's writings, perhaps by the hundred. He writes in *On Liberty*, "Human nature is not a machine to be built after a model, and set to do exactly the work prescribed for it, but a tree, which requires to grow and develop itself on all sides, according to the tendency of the inward forces which make it a living thing" (*OL*, pp. 56–57). Or again, "It is not by wearing down into uniformity all that is individual in themselves, but by cultivating it and calling it forth . . . that human beings become a noble and beautiful object of contemplation . . . " (*OL*, p. 60).

Even in his account of his education according to the principles of associationism, Mill acknowledges the existence of native tendencies.

> My course of study had led me to believe, that all mental and moral feelings and qualities, whether of a good or a bad kind, were the results of association. . . . [I]t now seemed to me, on retrospect, that my teachers had occupied themselves but superficially with the means of forming and keeping up these salutary associations. They seemed to have trusted altogether to the old familiar instruments, praise and blame, reward and punishment. Now, I did not doubt that by these means, begun early, and applied unremittingly, intense associations of pain and pleasure, especially of pain, might be created, and might produce desires and aversions capable of lasting undiminished to the end of life.

But there must always be something artificial and casual in associations thus produced. The pains and pleasures thus forcibly associated with things, are not connected with them by any natural tie. . . . (1873/1957a, pp. 88–90).

His "mental crisis," as he called it, was also mitigated by coming to the conclusion that our concern for the well-being of others is not just a product of association. There is a native propensity in human nature, he decided, to feel in unity with others, and this propensity can be nurtured in education. Association can be dissolved by analysis, but the feeling of sympathy for fellow human beings is rooted in human nature. He says it well in *Utilitarianism*:

> But moral associations which are wholly of artificial creation, when the intellectual culture goes on, yield by degrees to the dissolving force of analysis; and if the feeling of duty, when associated with utility, would appear equally arbitrary; if there were no leading department of our nature, no powerful class of sentiments, with which that association would harmonize, which would make us feel it congenial and incline us not only to foster it in others . . . , but also to cherish it in ourselves—if there were not, in short, a natural basis of sentiment for utilitarian morality, it might well happen that this association also, even after it had been implanted by education, might be analyzed away.
>
> But there *is* this basis of powerful natural sentiment. . . . This firm foundation is that of the social feelings of mankind—the desire to be in unity with our fellow creatures. . . . (1863/1957b, pp. 39–40)

In this instance, the associative process is not in competition with the original tendency, but reinforces it. The point, in any case, is that Mill explicitly recognizes a propensity of human nature that is not a product of association.

The social propensity can develop into altruism, a virtue that Mill held in highest esteem. In a remark that might have been made by Locke, Mill says, in *Utility of Religion*, "[T]he greatest thing which moral influences can do for the amelioration of human nature is to cultivate the unselfish feelings in the only mode in which any active principle can be effectually cultivated, namely, by habitual exercise . . . " (1874/1958a, p. 73). Equally Lockean remarks, such as the following, come from *On Liberty*: "The human faculties of perception, judgment, discriminative feeling, mental activity, and even moral preference are exercised only in making a choice. . . . The mental and the moral, like the muscular, powers are improved only by being used" (*OL*, p. 56). Mill does not refer to Locke in his discussions of education. In the *Autobiography*, however, he expresses great admiration for the educational theories of Pestalozzi. Mill fails to indicate what he liked in Pestalozzi, but the latter's pedagogy laid much store on the unfolding of the individual's inner nature.

In addition to quotations and references, which could be multiplied pedantically, there is further evidence of Mill's Lockean proclivities. Foremost, I think, are his repeated assertions that freedom is the *sine qua non* of human progress. *On Liberty* presses this theme throughout.[4] Such convictions are familiar to anyone who has read Mill's essays and books. Intellectual development is the condition of human progress; and intellectual development is dependent upon freedom. This is mining ore from Locke's mine. Humans have the inner resources to develop on their own, but they cannot do so under a tyranny. Set them free, and progress will follow. Freedom alone, without a specifically nurturing and formative environment, assures the effective development of human nature.

In chapter 2 of this volume there is a quotation from *On Liberty* to the effect that the individual mind can only flourish in an atmosphere of free inquiry and criticism. This does not mean for Mill, as it does for Dewey, that participation in intelligent practice *creates* habits of intelligence. It was observed in the same chapter that Mill judges public opinion to be the greatest threat to liberty. The problem with public opinion, Mill asserts, is that it is intimidating. Intimidation prevents the average intellect from being honestly and creatively exercised. Remove the intimidation (and provide a few geniuses for inspiration) and the individual intellect will flourish. Here again, the point is that freedom alone is sufficient for human growth.

Mill's political philosophy in general, whether found in *On Liberty*, *Considerations on Representative Government*, *The Principles of Political Economy*, or in numberless articles, reviews, and essays, always stresses the importance of freedom as absence of restraint—negative freedom, as mentioned above. *Political Economy*, for example, contains the following remark in the context of a discussion regarding the limits of government activity:

> The business of life is an essential part of the practical education of a people; without which, book and school instruction, though most necessary and salutary, does not suffice to qualify them for conduct, and for the adaptation of means to ends. Instruction is only one of the desiderata of mental improvement; another, almost as indispensable, is a vigorous exercise of the active energies; labour, contrivance, judgment, self control. . . . (1871/1965, p. 943)

In most instances, Mill believes it desirable to let people shift for themselves. Even his late socialism is individualistic. He has not come to regard society as an organism, in which the nature of each individual is an expression of his relationship to the whole. Antecedently autonomous individuals voluntarily engage in cooperative work and distribution of benefits. This will occur when the intellect and character of enough individuals have advanced far enough to make altruistic and cooperative behavior a general possibility. This advancement is presumably the result, at bottom, of liberty.

As the preceding remarks suggest, Mill does not believe that a struggle between separate individuals is a desirable form of society. He praises cooperation; and he hails experiments in economic cooperatives, believing that participation in such activities would develop unselfish habits. Here, on the educative function of activity, Mill sounds like Dewey. Another theme in Mill is the value of participating in public or common projects for the stimulus it provides to the growth of altruism.

> It is not sufficiently considered how little there is in most men's ordinary life to give any largeness either to their conceptions or to their sentiments. Their work is a routine; not a labor of love, but of self-interest in the most elementary form, the satisfaction of daily wants; neither the thing done nor the process of doing it introduces the mind to thoughts or feelings extending beyond individuals; if instructive books are within their reach, there is no stimulus to read them; and in most cases the individual has no access to any person of cultivation much superior to his own. Giving him something to do for the public supplies, in a measure, all these deficiencies. If circumstances allow the amount of public duty assigned to him to be considerable, it makes him an educated man. . . . He is called upon, while so engaged, to weigh interests not his own; to be guided, in case of conflicting claims, by another rule than his private partialities; to apply, at every turn, principles and maxims which have for their reason of existence the common good; and he usually finds associated with him in the same work minds more familiarized than his own with these ideas and operations, whose study it will be to supply reason to his understanding, and stimulation to his feeling for the general interest. He is made to feel himself one of the public, and whatever is for their benefit to be for his benefit. (Mill, 1861/1958b, pp. 53–54)

In this context, recall the doctrine of *Utilitarianism* that speaks of the social condition coming to feel completely natural to the individual. It is possible that Mill would consider such remarks to exemplify the associationist point of view. That would seem to be stretching the interpretation beyond tolerance, for he is in effect invoking the notion of experience and education as activity, and such a notion is not to be found in associationism. Perhaps, on the other side, such statements presuppose the theory of faculty psychology; and perhaps Mill is just saying that living in a particular kind of social environment gives one the opporunity to exercise his impartial and benevolent faculties.

For many of the statements that Mill makes about education, the reader cannot be sure what theory of education is presupposed.[5] Sometimes he will adopt different approaches to the identical problem. The virtue of altruism is always a concern for Mill. I quoted the remark from *Utility of Religion* to the effect that all we have to do is exercise this natural propensity. At other times, as in the *Autobiography*, Mill will invoke sensationalistic psychology and stress the importance of learning to associate pain with selfish actions. In *Auguste Comte and Positivism* he writes:

> It is as much a part of our scheme as of M. Comte's, that the direct cultivation of altruism, and the subordination of egoism to it, far beyond the point of absolute moral duty, should be one of the chief aims of education, both individual and collective. . . . We do not doubt that children and young persons will one day be again systematically disciplined in self-mortification; that they will be taught, as in antiquity, to control their appetites, to brave dangers, and submit voluntarily to pain, as simple exercises in education. Something has been lost as well as gained by no longer giving to every citizen the training necessary for a soldier. (1865/1961, p. 146)

> Until labourers and employers perform the work of industry in the spirit in which soldiers perform that of an army, industry will never be moralized, and military life will remain, what, in spite of the anti-social character of its direct object, it has hitherto been—the chief school of moral co-operation. (1865/1961, p. 149)

I assume that what Mill means here is the stern discipline of the military, in which failure to submit to authority or to subordinate one's personal interest to duty is met with certain, prompt, and severe penalties. Evidently associationist psychology is presupposed in this instance. (Inasmuch as Mill himself was highly altruistic and yet had no military experience, one wonders whether he thought of the education he had from his father as resembling military discipline.)

The analysis need not be taken further. The point is that Mill has at least two distinct and even incompatible philosophies of education, and maybe he even verges at times toward a third that resembles what was to be Dewey's. If one wanted to make an exhaustive analysis, I think he would find Mill also sounding on occasion like Plato in the latter's assumption that virtue is knowledge. A further source of insight might be Mill's insistence that less advanced societies should have different institutions and education than the more advanced ones. I have not found, however, that such inquiry dispels the basic ambiguity in Mill's philosophical anthropology.

The question of philosophy of education has been introduced because Mill as well as Dewey was seeking excellence in public discourse. Especially in *On Liberty*, Mill makes it sound rather easy; but this conclusion was sometimes as unsatisfactory to Mill as it was to Dewey.[6] Elsewhere he is conscious of the difficulty in educating citizens to the excellences necessary to make their discourse truly distinguished. Mill is always concerned with virtue, but he never makes it clear how we become virtuous.[7] He never develops a consistent philosophy of education. Contrary to the view that he was consistently an associationist, we have found that he unwittingly shuttles between that psychology and a Lockean position, in accordance with which the development of moral and intellectual powers is an essentially individual enterprise, provided the conditions of freedom are present.

Insofar as Mill represents Locke's philosophy, it is proper to regard him, technically, as an individualist. Dewey, then, is correct in part to call Mill an individualist, but he does so for the wrong reasons. Dewey does not identify Locke's philosophy of education in Mill. Had he done so, he would still have been critical, as he was of Locke. Dewey judges the notion of innate faculties to be mythical. Nothing is really explained or understood by saying that we remember because of the faculty of memory. That is saying that we remember because there is something about us that enables us to remember; but it tells us nothing about what it is or how it works. Dewey believes that we have native capacities, but they are not faculties. Of native tendencies he says, "Instead of being latent intellectual powers, requiring only exercise for their perfecting, they are tendencies to respond in certain ways to changes in the environment so as to bring about other changes" (1916, p. 68). True to his conviction that human nature and conduct are functions of interaction, he concludes, "Going to the root of the matter, the fundamental fallacy of the [Lockean] theory is its dualism; that is to say, its separation of activities and capacities [organism] from subject matter [environment]" (1916, p. 70). We should speak of habits rather than faculties, and the nature of a habit is determined by the organism and the environment together.

Accordingly, Dewey rejects the idea that freedom alone, negative freedom, is sufficient for human development. Growth, which is his idea of positive freedom, is a social product. Both in the classroom and in the experience of daily life, learning requires exacting attention to the environment, most especially to the quality of human relations. Those who are concerned with the development of human thought and character must find out how variations in the transactions between the individual and the environment determine human growth.

This is not to say that everything definitive in educational theory has been uttered by Dewey. It may even be that something can survive from Mill. Now it is suitable to attend more systematically to Dewey's ideas about excellence in democratic life, or, as he also calls it, social intelligence.

CHAPTER 5

Social Intelligence

Mill regards communication as an indispensable part of criticism and verification; but neither he nor any other philosopher has grasped the meaning of communication as fully as Dewey, who pursues richly and at length the hypothesis that communication in the context of activity is a necessary condition of meaningful experience and of the formation and development of mind. He provides many technical analyses of the phenomenon of language. In addition to basic theoretical studies, he writes of both the practical virtues of communication and the intrinsic delight of shared experience.

> Of all affairs, communication is the most wonderful. That things should be able to pass from the plane of external pushing and pulling to that of revealing themselves to man, and thereby to themselves; and that the fruit of communication should be participation, sharing, is a wonder by the side of which transubstantiation pales. (1925a, p. 132)

> Shared experience is the greatest of human goods. In communication, such conjunction and contact as is characteristic of animals become endearments capable of infinite idealization; they become symbols of the very culmination of nature. That God is love is a more worthy idealization than that the divine is power. Since love at its best brings illumination and wisdom, this meaning is as worthy as that the divine is truth. (1925a, pp. 157–58)

> Apart from conversation, from discourse and communication, there is no thought and no meaning, only just events, dumb, preposterous, destructive. (1922a, p. 280)

Communication is central to democratic life. Dewey frequently uses the expression "democracy as a way of life." The casual reader, I find, makes the error of assuming that Dewey is discussing the political process exclusively. The same reader then leaps to the conclusion that Dewey wanted to politicize every dimension of shared experience. Dewey had no such intent; he had a healthy fear of big government. Democracy as a way of life prevails when participants in associated life carry on their relationships by means of communication pervaded with mutual respect and regard. These relationships would of course include political processes, but they would include all manner of human associations as well. Indeed, the habits, or virtues, of being democratic constitute a moral norm for the individual in all his behavior. "We have advanced far enough to say that democracy is a way of life. We have yet to realize that it is a way of personal life and one which provides a moral standard for personal conduct" (Dewey, 1939/1963a, p. 130).

He was convinced that political democracy could not function effectively without the habits that would be developed in the wider domain of personal relationships.

> The real trouble is that there is an intrinsic split in our habitual attitudes when we profess to depend upon discussion and persuasion in politics and then systematically depend upon other methods in reaching conclusions in matters of morals and religion, or in anything where we depend upon a person or group possessed of "authority." We do not have to go to theological matters to find examples. In homes and schools, the places where the essentials of character are supposed to be formed, the usual procedure is settlement of issues, intellectual and moral, by appeal to the "authority" of parent, teacher, or textbook. Dispositions formed under such conditions are so inconsistent with the democratic method that in a crisis they may be aroused to act in positively anti-democratic ways for anti-democratic ends. . . . (Dewey, 1939/1963a, p. 129)

Dewey less frequently uses "social intelligence" than "democracy," but "social intelligence" is less misleading. The focus of the present inquiry is narrower than democracy as a way of life. We are concerned with excellence in public discourse. It must be remembered, however, that such excellence can be actual only to the extent that democracy as a way of life is actual. The process of social intelligence as a model of public discourse will be elaborated momentarily. Let us first take note of the sorts of considerations that prompted Dewey to develop his philosophy in this direction. He examines this issue more deeply than Mill had done.

He is firmly persuaded that there is no fixed and final criterion of moral judgment. In this he opposes the classic tradition. The philosophers of the classic tradition had assumed that being in its essential nature is changeless and perfect. Hence the nature of being, once it is known, is an infallible and indisputable moral standard. Plato's philosophy is the paradigm. There is an eternal and immutable form of the good; likewise of the just; and there is a full array of additional essences. The perfect city is one that is patterned after the eternal order; the perfect individual is one whose soul replicates that same order. In judging any action, we must compare it to the antecedently existing archetypes of cosmic perfection.

Philosophers have taken Plato's example seriously. They have looked for the eternal and unchanging and used it as the foundation for their moral system. Theories of natural law, divine command, the categorical imperative, and the invariant dialectic of class struggle are some examples. In Dewey's youth, the proponents of philosophical idealism defended the view that the cosmic spirit manifests itself in the state, and the duty of the citizen is therefore to conform to his antecedently given station in the social order. The classical liberals believed that the institutions of laissez-faire capitalism represent the true order of nature.[1] In every case, there is an antecedently fixed order or principle of some kind, and moral conduct consists in conforming to it.

Suppose all these claims are a myth, an unwitting concoction of some author? On the face of it, the claims are implausible, because they differ significantly from one another. Many people believe that religious teachings provide certain and unexceptionable prescriptions for conduct. This would be easier to believe if there were not such great moral diversity within and between religious communities. If absolutist claims are unfounded, conformity to them amounts to unquestioning obedience to some particular human authority. Adherence to timeless and perfect moral dictates is actually conformity to the demands of a certain culture, or an elite within it.

Dewey finds no credibility in the arguments for immutable being, and he thinks that the evidence of modern science points unmistakably to the conclusion that all things are in a process of change. Einstein had demolished the view that the universe is composed of fixed substances, and before that Darwin had presented conclusive evidence that all living things evolve. It was no longer credible to regard human reason as a changeless faculty with special access to eternal truth. Dewey consequently opposes the classic tradition in all its manifestations, principally because he thought it smothered inquiry into the possibilities of human fulfillment.

While many of the demands cloaked in religious and philosophic garb have been stultifying and sometimes barbaric, many others have not. By means of a stunning array of philosophical and theological arguments, every society has demanded, in general, the elementary behavior needed for preserving social order: participating in work, caring for children and educating them, refraining from murder, theft, and other forms of violence, keeping agreements, telling the truth, and suchlike. What Dewey objects to is regarding such principles as beyond exception, criticism, or refinement:

> Principles exist as hypotheses with which to experiment. Human history is long. There is a long record of experimentation in conduct, and there are cumulative verifications which give many principles a well earned prestige. Lightly to disregard them is the height of foolishness. . . . [T]he choice is not between throwing away rules previously developed and sticking obstinately by them. The intelligent alternative is to revise, adapt, expand and alter them. (1922b, pp. 164–65)

The experimental point of view does not mean that we cannot be intensely opposed to murder, or passionately attached to freedom or to the institution of the family. We can nevertheless raise important questions about these issues. Is the death penalty desirable? Euthanasia? Abortion? When is war justifiable? What are the appropriate limitations of freedom? Do we want to require everyone to be in a family? What kinds of families are injurious to their members, and when might we interfere in the privacy of families where violence occurs? What particular forms of family life are beneficial to their members, and what variations in family structure might be desirable? And so on. It is sometimes believed that human beings cannot form powerful loyalties unless they suspend their critical intelligence. It happens all too often that our attachments *are* formed in just that way, but it need not be so. We are passionate beings and have strong commitments in any case. There is no necessity that commitments remain unqualified, and there is no reason why our passions cannot be directed to goals clarified by intelligent examination. How strong, for example, can a friendship be that cannot endure change?

In many of its forms, the classic tradition had also insisted on the notion that there is a hierarchy of being, or reality. Plato's *Republic*, for example, distinguished five levels (including the Good, which was identified as "beyond being"). At the same time, individuals have no reality *as individuals*. They exist only as an exemplification of the universal, which does have reality. What we call *individuals* have reality only as members of a class. Dewey believes that such notions of hierarchy serve as a justification for creating hierarchies in human society that exploit and exclude whole classes of humans as nonpersons. Slaves are "really" subhuman. Women as women are insufficiently competent and intelligent to engage in business, politics, scholarship, and the arts. Blacks as blacks are incapable of autonomy; workers as workers are unfit for anything but physical labor. When it has been defended at all, human exploitation has typically been rationalized by way of such generalizations: The excluded or subservient classes are said to belong in the order of being at an inherently inferior level. In reply to such arguments, Dewey writes:

> Now whatever the idea of equality means for democracy, it means, I take it, that the world is not to be construed as a fixed order of species, grades or degrees. It means that every existence deserving the name of existence has something unique and irreplaceable about it, that it does not exist to illustrate a principle, to realize a universal or to embody a kind or class. (1919, p. 52)

Another of the presuppositions of Dewey's philosophy of democracy is his pluralism, which is derivative of his very conception of philosophy. Nothing in his thought is more fundamental than his assumption that philosophic theory must be subordinate to experience.[2] Philosophy describes and elucidates life experience and its potentialities; it does not obscure or deny them. Dewey says the worst fault in philosophies is what he calls "selective emphasis": the selection of one feature of experience and the subsequent assumption that it is the *only* feature. (One of many examples of this is the assumption that the nature of being is exhausted in its mathematical properties.) A moral philosophy, accordingly, would not deny the existence of the plurality of kinds of moral value. Dewey argues that there is an irreducible plurality of moral criteria. He distinguishes three (a modest number, actually): there are ends, rights and duties, and standards of virtue and vice. He calls these alternately "independent factors" or "independent variables," and he argues that none of them can be reduced to the others; nor is there a fixed priority among them. We can always try to adjust and unite these considerations in a moral situation, but there can be no assurance that they will not be in conflict. There can be conflicts, for example, between the right and the good, with no uncontroversial way to determine which takes precedence. This is Dewey's summary:

> In the face of the role played by the real conflict of forces in moral situations and the manifest uncertainty about which side [among these

forces] to take, I am inclined to think that one of the causes of the ineffi-
ciency of moral theories resides in their attachment to the unitary concept, which has led them to simplify moral life excessively. The result is
an abyss between the involved realities of practice and the abstract forms
of the system. A moral philosophy which frankly recognizes the impossibility of reducing all the elements of moral situations to one single
principle, one which would admit that every human being can only do
his best to shift for himself among the disparate forces, would throw
light on our real difficulties and would help us make a more accurate
estimate of competing factors. It would be necessary to sacrifice the idea
that there exists, theoretically and beforehand, a unique and ideally correct solution for every difficulty into which a person will be thrown.
(1930b, p. 204)

Characteristically, Dewey adds:

Personally, I believe that this sacrifice, far from being a loss, would be a
gain. By turning our attention from rigid rules and standards, it would
lead us to take fuller consideration of the specific elements which
necessarily enter into every situation where we must act. (1930b, p. 204)[3]

We have already noted Dewey's clear perception of the social dimension of scientific inquiry. From this perception, and from what he
thought of as the collapse of the classic tradition, it is an easy step to
the conviction that ethical discourse can likewise be inherently social.
The isolated individual is powerless in scientific and moral situations
alike. Only in communication can the deficiencies of the individual
intelligence be corrected, its powers developed, fulfilled, and made
effective. No one is perfectly good or perfectly wise. Any particular
moral conviction is always subject to revision, rejection, or expansion. Dewey is as aware as Mill or Peirce of human fallibility, and he
equally agrees that disciplined communication is the principal
remedy for our limitations. In a remark that might have been written
by Mill, Dewey says "capacity to endure publicity and communication is the test by which it is decided whether a pretended good is
spurious or genuine" (1920, p. 197). Bearing all such considerations
in mind, Dewey seizes upon social intelligence as the evident answer
to the age-long quest for a method to bring human beings voluntarily
into greater accord.

The occasion for social intelligence as public discourse is the occurrence of a problem implicating the public or some segment of it.
Some sort of obstacle, conflict, or perplexity has been perceived, and
we must determine what to do about it. It could be a massive problem
of foreign affairs, such as United States policy in Central America; or

it could be a parochial question, like the proposal to build an expressway through a residential area. There is uncertainty, conflict, and disagreement. There are divergent interests to be reconciled or adjusted. In such a case, Dewey urges, we should address the problem with honest, intelligent, and creative communication.

This means first that the parties to the controversy must engage in inquiry to determine the nature of their problematic situation. They must find out just what needs and conditions have created the impasse. What is the need for the expressway, for example? And precisely what would be the impact of the road on the existing neighborhood? At this point in an actual controversy, the various parties would be viewing each other with suspicion and alarm; and in all probability they would have jumped to conclusions about who was exploiting whom, or who was obstructing progress, or who is public spirited and who is motivated by private lust. They would surely have very different views about the cause of the problem and about the changes that the proposed road would bring about. Passions would be running high, with no one in a conciliatory mood.

Let us assume that a real need for the road can be demonstrated. Perhaps it would minimize traffic congestion and driving hazards. It might save not just time but lives. Perhaps, too, it would facilitate trade and commerce and create new employment opportunities. For their part, the residents of the area would evidently have added noise, litter, air pollution, and hazard to pedestrians. They believe that their property values would decline; and they fear there would be rezoning, bringing with it fast-food outlets, commercial enterprises, and greater population density. The aesthetic qualities of the neighborhood might well be destroyed: In place of trees, lawns, parks, and winding roads there might be bridges, overpasses, embankments, masses of concrete, and incessant clatter.

But these assumptions cannot be taken for granted. The facts must be determined by inquiry. The first phase of a democratic solution would be to engage in the inquiry. The initial passions of the disputants are not to be trusted. Certainly the inquiry would proceed from many directions. It would not be facilitated by muttered threats and curses, or by public name-calling and recrimination. If the affected persons take the inquiry seriously, their attitudes might well change in some ways. Perhaps the zeal of the road builders will subside when they discover how hurtful the road will be, and they will look for an alternative. Or the local people will discover that the plans for the road are much less injurious than originally assumed. Our evaluations of a situation change as our understanding of the nature of the situation changes; but we cannot get even that far if we are determined to hold on to our initial prejudices.

It would be a mistake to assume that the situation could be resolved only by accepting the solution offered either by the road-builders or by the local citizens. There will almost certainly be alternatives that no one has yet contrived. The values at issue might be satisfied in another plan. Perhaps the design features of the road need not be nearly so obnoxious as the homesteaders initially feared, and the homeowners might be convinced that the transportation needs are so great that some interference in their environment might be justified. Or maybe the roadway can be constructed on another route; or an improved bus system might be the solution.

In determining the nature of the problematic situation and in conceiving of possible solutions to it, there can be no substitute for the actual participation of the parties involved. If real human beings are somehow affected by change and the possibility of change, in the final analysis only they can say just how they are affected and how intensely. Likewise, only they can judge whether a particular plan of action is acceptable. They would be well advised to bring in experts to advise them of the costs and consequences of different options and of the technical feasibility of different plans. In the present example, some smart engineers and landscape architects might work wonders in pointing out new possibilities. But the role of the expert, Dewey cautions, is to advise, not to decide.

Coming to some kind of an agreement here would be greatly assisted if the persons facing each other had some respect for each other's values and some mutual trust. If the roadbuilders really do not care about the damage done to neighborhoods, the chances of accommodation are nil. Likewise, if the local community cares nothing for the needs of the larger community, a compromise may be impossible. On the other hand, if all sides can safely address each other as persons who genuinely seek a common solution, real progress might be made.

In virtually any consultative process, the values at issue are numerous and diverse; and even after extended and even-handed discussion, disagreements remain. This is a common fact of experience. The to-build-or-not-to-build controversy has no perfect solution, and perhaps it remains stymied. At that point, perhaps, the defenders of the road might take final recourse in appeal to the general utility of their proposal, while the local residents might well ask by what right their lives and homes can be invaded for the convenience of motorists. They might defend themselves by appealing to property rights. After all that inquiry and collaborative deliberation, a moral disagreement remains. What can social intelligence, as Dewey conceives it, do for such a standoff?

In many ways Dewey's position is like that of Mill, who insists that any view that we hold is open to revision and that the principal instrument for correcting and improving our opinions is to submit them to a social test. In the immediate context, the pertinence of Dewey's denial of absolutes is that neither the utility claimed by the roadbuilders nor the rights claimed by the property owners can be regarded as a definitive and final appeal to the moral conflict. Utility is one of the conspicuous values in the moral life, but it is not exclusive. In the experience of many, for example, what we call *rights* are sometimes held to take priority over utility, and likewise with duties. Hence I might believe that someone to whom I have made a solemn promise has more claim on my actions than persons with whom I have no ties. Accordingly, I might make a marginal increase in the aggregate pleasure by taking some kids to a ballgame; but if I have made a promise to my friend to help him clean his garage, this promise takes precedence even if the aggregate pleasure is less. When I spend large sums of money for the health of my family, I am using funds that might well bring greater happiness if spent on antibiotics for children in South America. In such an instance, the specific obligation to my family and their explicit expectations of me take precedence, for me, over what might turn out to be the claims of utility. The utilitarian, of course, will challenge these judgments; but the challenge seems to beg the question. It presupposes rather than proves that utility is the only valid criterion.

One party can continue to give exclusive priority to rights and the other to utility. In Dewey's analysis, both positions are reductive. They are selecting one of a plurality of moral values and claiming that it alone has moral authority.[4] As long as one side insists absolutely on utility and the other side is equally intransigent about rights, then no solution will ever be found. Dewey counsels such disputants to reconsider their steadfast allegiances. They have no warrant for judging their criteria to be absolute, and their inflexibility makes any solution short of violence impossible.

It may be that no solution is forthcoming in any case. Dewey makes no guarantees that there will. But he believes it is much more likely that we can reach intersubjective moral agreement, and hence adjust and unite our aims, if we are willing to consider that the other person's moral values might have some merit. He or she, too, must think the same way about us. All of us might consider it possible to revise or qualify our convictions in some way. Then it is at least possible that some agreement can be reached, where before it was not. It is widely believed that possessing moral absolutes facilitates moral agreement. This would be true, I suppose, if everyone held the same absolutes; but they do not. This is not a war of absolutes between the children of light and the children of darkness. Sister and brother, husband and wife, friends and neighbors do not take precisely the same position regarding such issues as the death penalty, abortion, mercy killing, private property, free speech, sexual behavior, and so on. If we were all absolutists, we could rarely agree about anything.

However, the obvious plurality of moral values need not be an impediment to the increase of moral concord. Dewey, as we have seen, concludes that there is a plurality of basic moral criteria. At the same time he argues that they are antagonistic only infrequently; and he points out that conflicts between them are not usually oppositions of good and evil, but of positive but incommensurable values.

Pluralism in moral experience can be given an additional, and I think very helpful, formulation. There is probably not one moral issue about which all the readers of these pages would *precisely* agree. It might be the death penalty, abortion, animal rights, Central American policy—think of any case you wish. Those who favor abortion under some circumstances will differ concerning just what those circumstances should be. Those who are against it will not be perfectly agreed either. They might differ, for example, on just how severe a moral evil it is. This difference would show up in different prescriptions for preventing or punishing abortions. The other cases will provoke similar differences. We will all regard murder as indefensible, I presume; but we will differ as to just what constitutes murder. Is abortion murder? The death penalty? Euthanasia? Any killing whatever? And again we will differ on how seriously to treat the crime. We might reduce murder very greatly, for example, by permitting the police to detain anyone who looked the least bit suspicious. How far will we go in reducing freedom in order to reduce the incidence of murder? There can be no perfect agreement. Yet, even though we do not agree precisely about anything, we are no doubt capable of constituting a more or less effective moral community. Our differences are not great enough to convert pluralism into mayhem. There is a simple reason for this: The benefits of mutual tolerance, cooperation, and friendship vastly outweigh whatever benefits there might be in distrust, interference, and antagonism. There are few persons, if any, who are absolutely intolerant of any moral values not identical to their own. Otherwise, we are all pluralists, differing only in the degree of our tolerance.

If individuals are sufficiently possessed of the democratic virtues, greater levels of harmony are possible with neither coercion nor moral cowardice. The imagined case of the road (to get back to that again) could remain stalemated indefinitely, but if it were ever to be resolved on a moral basis, the chances for success would seem to be a function of the willingness of the participants to commit themselves to a genuinely cooperative procedure.

The method of social intelligence addresses social problems experimentally. Unquestioning obedience to authority is rejected. Fixation on absolutes—whether those of ethical theory, religion, custom, or tradition—is likewise rejected. No one (to revert to Mill's phraseology) regards himself as infallible, with nothing to learn from others and with inherent authority to decide matters unilaterally. The persons engaged in a morally problematic situation would, ideally, engage in common analysis and inquiry. They would collaborate to define their problem and its causes. There would be communication and consultation to determine the values at issue. All sides would be heard fully and impartially. Reservations and criticisms would be exchanged, and all would share in the formulation of novel plans of action. These in turn would be evaluated, rejected, or revised until the possibility of concerted action finally occurred. This is not a power struggle or an adversarial situation. It is a common effort. The discourse that typifies such a process would presumably resemble the sort that Mill speaks of at the conclusion of chapter II of *On Liberty*. It would not be rude, abusive, deceptive, uninformed, or dogmatic; it would welcome contributions from all concerned, and it would consider them conscientiously.

The example I have been developing is paradigmatic of social intelligence. It is a relatively small-scale problem. For his own part, Dewey gives his attention to matters of wider scope, such as national and international economic policy, issues of war and peace, civil rights, education, and academic freedom.[5] Dewey thinks of himself as a participant in the dialogue addressed to such questions, not as a final authority; and he wants the democratic public to be equally a participant. He recognizes that issues of national public policy are more complex and difficult than matters of road construction in residential communities. He is likewise aware that the public is unprepared to deal with these controversies intelligently. Local communities endure stresses originating far beyond their borders in time and space. We live in an environment that is deeply disturbed by forces that are very difficult to recognize, much less understand. The relatively simple days of the nineteenth century have given way to massive industrialization, rapid urban growth, telephones, telegraph, airplanes, world wars, and finally nuclear weapons. "The local face-to-face community has been invaded by forces so vast, so remote in initiation, so far-reaching in scope and so complexly indirect in operation, that they are, from the standpoint of the members of local social units, unknown" (Dewey, 1927, p. 316).q The public is dazed, bewildered, aimless, and consequently apathetic as well. Most citizens want nothing to do with politics. The problems, then, of initiating excellence in public discourse are staggering, as Dewey well knows. He has many proposals for doing something about it, and we will take note of them later in the chapter. There are some philosophical issues to attend to first.

Perhaps the reader thinks there is nothing radical or even problematic about social intelligence as the method of public discourse; but it is radical and problematic. I remarked in the discussion of Mill that his plea to make moral discourse an inherently communicative process had extremely little precedent in the history of philosophy, and that the idea had not caught on with his successors, until it reappears in Dewey. Dewey does not succeed in altering the philosophic landscape in this regard either. Moral philosophy since Dewey has still tended very much to oscillate between forms of absolutism and subjectivism; and in any case it has been individualistic.

In recent years the books in moral philosophy that have received the most attention are by John Rawls (1971), Robert Nozick (1974), Ronald Dworkin (1976), Alan Gewirth (1978), and Alasdair MacIntyre (1984).6 The idea of social intelligence as normative method has no place in any of these works. Rawls contrives an "original position," as he calls it, which is populated by equally contrived beings. They have no self-knowledge whatsoever and no moral convictions. On the other hand, they have more knowledge of human nature and human behavior than is possessed by any living person. These beings create a contract that establishes principles of justice "once and for all." The persons of nature and history—such as you and I—have no authority to change any of the provisions of the contract, no matter what the consequences of the contract, no matter how uniform is our agreement, no matter how urgent our desire for change. Nozick postulates a state of nature with certain absolute rights, and he determines how the political state would arise from that condition. For Nozick, too, the aims and values of actual historical beings are irrelevant. Dworkin believes there exists a universal right to equal concern and respect. He thinks it is axiomatic, and he believes we may deduce

qSee Appendix B, p. 132.

specific rights from it that will exactly determine the right answer to disagreements about public policy. Gewirth postulates a "perfectly rational" agent whose basic moral thinking is unencumbered by any historical accretions or considerations. While MacIntyre does insist that historical considerations must be introduced into moral thinking, he is nevertheless confident that at a given historical period it is possible to determine a moral end that will be exclusively authoritative in respect to moral judgment and conduct. Like all the other persons mentioned in this paragraph, he regards moral pluralism as a degenerate condition.

These texts have much of interest in them, and they deserve thorough critical analysis. My intent is to point out that each purports to establish an indisputable moral norm—a norm that would be impervious to the historical workings of social intelligence. A kind of absolutistic position is deliberately taken in each instance. In my judgment, each of these arguments has fatal weaknesses. The key in Rawls, for example, is the formation of the original position and its inhabitants—everything depends on it. This allegedly timeless condition is a product of what Rawls calls "our considered judgments." But whose judgments are these, really, that determine what the initial choice conditions are to be? They are highly unrepresentative of the moral convictions of many—indeed, most—conscientious persons. Surely they are not timeless, but local. Thus Rawls would convert the spirit of the age in a rather tiny subculture into universal truth. Nozick's state of nature is presented without supportive argument, and it takes no heed of the needs and values that go into the formation of actual political states. Dworkin's contention that there is a universal right to equal concern and respect is groundless. He could more intelligibly say there *ought* to be such a right. Even then, however, it would by no means be clear what would follow from such a right. Dworkin's so-called deductions are not exercises in logic, but evaluations. The rights he invokes in his analyses of public policy issues do not follow logically from the alleged fundamental right to equal concern and respect, because it is a matter of moral judgment to determine what constitutes such respect. He, too, cloaks the spirit of the age in a rationalistic disguise. Similar problems arise with the other works mentioned. The classic tradition lives! The love of the eternal and unchanging has resurfaced with such writings. Whether their observance would be beneficial in actual societies is another question.

Such a rapid survey cannot be taken as conclusive, of course; but perhaps it can raise doubts about the validity of the very enterprise of establishing unquestionable moral principles. Philosophies of this sort might be more convincing if they agreed with each other; but there is in fact heated controversy between them. Moreover, the debate does not move them closer together. Our history does not provide the slightest evidence that there will be moral unanimity in either theory or practice. This seems to illustrate the futility of absolutism.

The philosophies under review are in an obvious sense individualistic. The work of a single individual is (naively) presented as a product of timeless and impersonal reason, and it is assumed to be normative for the rest of us. In each instance the author seems to distinguish what is in fact most important to him, and he then constructs a theory in order to absolutize it. The method of absolutizing is to articulate some sort of ideal conditions of choice, or perhaps to define a perfectly rational agent, or define the perfection of human nature. For better or worse, however, there seems to be no rational way to coerce agreement about what constitutes "ideal" choice conditions or "perfect" rationality. There are no perfect solutions. I know what constitutes a "perfect" solution, of course, but it turns out that my idea of perfection is unlike yours. If I believe, nevertheless, that I possess the true idea of perfection, I am tempted to impose it on you, regardless of your protests. This is exactly what Rawls and Nozick, for example, would do. These people make social intelligence look so liberating!

Among contemporary philosophers of note, there is one whose thoughts on the moral functions of discourse appear to be very similar to those of Mill and Dewey. This is Jürgen Habermas, who follows more from the Marxian than from liberal tradition. I think the resemblance to Mill and Dewey is highly deceptive, and I believe both would reject Habermas's position. In note number 6 in the present chapter I have devoted a paragraph to a summary account and critique of Habermas's conclusions.

Coexisting with those of perfect moral certitude are those who claim that there are no objective grounds for making any distinction whatsoever between competing moral claims. For such persons, then, there is no point at all in engaging in discourse, for the whole enterprise is in vain. This is a position taken more often in theory than in practice. Moral problems occur in a definite context; there is a specific disagreement, a specific social conflict. Therefore there are specific values at issue. They are somehow incompatible or at variance. Thus there are definite issues to be reflected upon, investigated, and negotiated.

One might turn his back on such problems by making the assumption that no one has any legitimate claims to press on anyone else. Dewey might well put the matter in just the opposite terms, by urging that everyone has a legitimate, if provisional, claim. He rejects the notion, found in the classic tradition and elsewhere, that there are some individuals who have priority over others just by virtue of the fact that they exist. Likewise there are no persons who may make no claims just because of their class or group status. A kind of moral equality is consistent with the natural condition of mankind. This means that you have no right to exploit me and I have none to exploit you. It means that both your claims and mine are equally entitled to a hearing. Such equality demands a certain impartiality: There cannot be one rule for you and another for me.

All this is very abstract and philosophical. In ordinary life most of us learn quite readily that if we try to make an exception of ourselves, others will not tolerate it. They will ask, "What makes you so special?" If we are fortunate, we discover that it is better for us to function with others as equals. We are social beings, and we require the support and cooperation of others in the pursuit of our aims. One can try, of course, to function as an isolated atom, but such efforts typically fail. Or one might try to act in deliberate concert with others. Dewey, like Mill, is confident that such behavior is inherently more satisfying than cultivating antagonisms. Occasionally, of course, groups of individuals do succeed in dominating others. No doubt they enjoy it to some extent; but any moral justification of their status must be cloaked in mythology.

Saying this much does not take us very far in solving specific moral problems. Moral impartiality does not mean that all differences in role, status, and reward are ruled out. Assent to impartiality does not prohibit inequalities of wealth, power, and authority, which might be justified on such grounds as utility, desert, or agreement, to name just three. We are apt to differ on what is justified. Although moral equality forbids the exclusion of women just because they are women, it does not determine what the criteria are for determining who is entitled to a given position in society. Hence we might have a conscientious difference as to whether this particular person, who happens to be a woman, has a warranted claim to this particular employment. The coexistence of moral impartiality and moral pluralism is one of the principal sources of our ethical dilemmas. Insofar as I respect the values of different individuals, and insofar as these values are in conflict, then I am caught in divergent loyalties. In such instances, one would hope that the contending parties were not absolutists!

Social intelligence commends itself in the situation of moral equality just because of the indeterminateness of that condition. It neither postulates a social vacuum governed by *a priori* imperatives nor takes the position of extreme relativism and nihilism. It recognizes the existence of a plurality of moral values operative in any situation, and it provides assumptions and methods for criticizing, adjusting, uniting, and enlarging them in a specific plan of action. It is moral pluralism become intelligent and respectful of itself. Insofar as it is possible to attain intersubjective moral agreement and to attain voluntary union in conduct, social intelligence appears superior to its alternatives.

The discussion of the last few paragraphs was occasioned by the thought that social intelligence might seem a commonplace. I have been suggesting (a) that it is by no means commonplace, there being various rivals to it as moral method and (b) that it is preferable to its alternatives. Another question might arise: Is this democratic procedure really what Dewey has in mind as the means of addressing ethical issues?

This question arises because of Dewey's obsession with incorporating scientific method into ethical discourse. Most scholars have assumed that Dewey intended to *reduce* ethics to some manner of science. They have assumed that a moral problem would be treated exactly like a scientific problem and would be solved just like one. Accordingly (so the scholars have thought), we would have scientifically verifiable definitions of 'good', 'right', and so on; and we could therefore prove that a given action was good or bad just as we prove that water boils at 212 degrees Fahrenheit or that bodies attract each other directly with the mass and inversely with the square of the distance between them.[7]

This is not what Dewey has in mind. Scientific method and knowledge would be extremely useful in the moral life, to be sure, but not exhaustive of it. By means of science we can learn the conditions of many human goods and evils, and we can consequently do something about them, rather than leave them to chance. We can also be scientific by having a will to inquiry, open mindedness, and experiment, rather than by being dogmatic and intolerant. The scientific spirit, as Dewey understands it, would also show itself in the formation of experimental hypotheses for novel reconstructions of problematic situations, rather than in obedience to precedent. Most important of all, moral inquiry would be like scientific inquiry in that it would be collaborative, social.

Even when we have used all the resources of science, there will still be disagreements about what to do. We can agree about all the facts of the case, and we can share what information we have about possible solutions to it. That does not mean that we will have equal approval of each solution, no matter how morally earnest we are.

Complementary resources are needed. The strictly scientific procedure gradually incorporates additional virtues. It is not clear in Dewey just where science becomes nonscience, but making an exact division is not important. In a morally problematic situation governed by the norms of democratic intelligence, each person would consider it possible to be persuaded to modify the convictions with which he or she began. This is a scientific virtue, presumably, but it is extended to the moral domain. Ideally, everyone would also have respect and tolerance for the values of others and would wish to be supportive of them. One feels the pull in another's outlook and has some sympathy for it. Here we seem to be talking about virtues that are distinguishable from the attitudes necessary for strictly scientific inquiry, but certainly indispensable for intersubjective moral agreement.

To use the language of Aristotle, we need both moral and intellectual virtues in the moral life. That is, while ethics can make great use of science, scientific method, and scientific attitudes, it is not reducible to these. While the democratic virtues borrow much from the scientific spirit, they are also something more than that. Dewey is famous for his arguments that we should use science in the moral life. He is also famous for being the foremost American philosopher of democracy. There are not two Deweys here, but one; and scholars who ignore one side of Dewey miss the wisdom in his philosophy.

Dewey must shoulder part of the blame for confusions in interpretation. While he has many systematic studies concerning the nature and implications of experimental science, he has no comparable analyses of moral virtue. There is great insight expressed on the general nature of virtue in his *Ethics* of 1932 (pp. 255–60), but there are no full-scale treatments.[8] Lack of clarity is evident in his careless use of language, for example. Sometimes he uses "democratic" to denote the sum of human excellences, but at other times he uses "intelligent" to the same purpose. On still other occasions he uses "scientific attitude" to refer to the collection of virtues required for democratic life. Lacking a single discussion in which all such notions are clarified and interrelated, scholars, not surprisingly, have not captured the entirety of Dewey's philosophy.

Nevertheless, the substance of his position is clear. Saying that the extension of the scientific attitude is indispensable to the survival of democracy, Dewey lists some of its distinctive characteristics: "willingness to hold belief in suspense, ability to doubt until evidence is obtained; willingness to go where evidence points instead of putting first a personally preferred conclusion; ability to hold ideas in solution and use them as hypotheses to be tested instead of dogmas to be asserted; and . . . enjoyment of new fields for inquiry and of new problems" (1939/1963a, p. 145)ʳ Taking a more inclusive view, he says "Democracy is a *personal* way of individual life; . . . it signifies the possession and continual use of certain attitudes, forming personal character and determining desire and purpose in all the relations of life" (1940, p. 222).ˢ

Scattered through a considerable variety of writings, we find him affirming that the moral life cannot exist on experimental norms and scientific method alone. There are many personal qualities to which he draws our attention rather unsystematically: Sympathy, kindliness, sincerity, tolerance, creativity, imaginativeness, impartiality, conscientiousness, flexibility, independence, initiative, integrity, and courage are some of the virtues he commends to us. If the following remarks were analyzed, they would reveal a whole catalogue of qualities essential to public discourse at its finest: Faith in democracy, Dewey writes,

> may be enacted in statutes, but it is only on paper unless it is put in force in the attitudes which human beings display to one another in all the incidents and relations of daily life. To denounce Naziism for intolerance, cruelty, and stimulation of hatred amounts to fostering insincerity if in our . . . relations to other persons, . . . we are moved by racial, color, or . . . class prejudice. . . . Intolerance, abuse, calling of names because of differences of opinion about religion or politics or business, as well as because of differences of race, color, wealth, or degree of culture, are treason to the democratic way of life. . . . Merely legal guarantees of the civil liberties of free belief, free expression, free assembly are of little avail if in daily life freedom of communication, the give and take of ideas, facts, experiences, is choked by mutual suspicion, by abuse, by fear and hatred.
>
> . . . Democracy is the belief that even when needs and ends . . . are different for each individual, the habit of amicable cooperation . . . is itself a priceless addition to life. To take as far as possible every conflict which arises . . . out of the atmosphere and medium of force . . . into that of discussion and of intelligence, is to treat those who disagree . . . with us as those from whom we may learn, and in so far, as friends. (1940, pp. 223–26)ᵗ

ʳSee Appendix B, p. 118.
ˢSee Appendix B, p. 148.

ᵗSee Appendix B, pp. 149–50.

This is a plea much like Mill's in *On Liberty*, but expressed more personally.

In talking about the habits constituting the scientific morale, Dewey observes, "Every one of these traits goes contrary to some human impulse that is naturally strong" (1939/1963a, p. 146).[u] It is very difficult to acquire the habits that would give excellence to our communication. This is a challenge not only to our schools, but to all our institutions. As noted before, learning is most effective, Dewey believes, when it is active rather than passive. Schooling should not put its emphasis on filling young minds with masses of predigested information, which is then to be returned much in the form in which it was received. The emphasis in learning must be on *inquiry*, with all the skills and attitudes cognate to it. This is not the neglect of subject matter; it is the aggressive and exciting approach to it, which at the same time makes the intellect an effective power. Students may learn history, for example, by memorizing names and dates from a text; or they may learn it by approaching historical subject matter as problematic and hence as demanding inquiry. Students may be *taught*, say, the presumed causes of the American Civil War; or they may see the problem of the onset of the War as an occasion for inquiry. Curiosity is more likely to be aroused, imagination must be used to formulate hypotheses, and active effort must be made to test hypotheses and achieve discovery. The results of different inquiries must be actively considered, and the learners will undergo the experience of suspending judgment, weighing evidence, and revising assumptions. Why could not a history course be designed after this manner? Why could not the instructor be as much a guide to inquiry as an authority on the subject matter?

Schooling in America, Dewey thought, has had an inherently conservative purpose: to teach people to respect the status quo and to be prepared to accept one's role in it. He is confident that a radically different pedagogy would stimulate the development of critical and creative intelligence well beyond the achievement of existing schools; and that this intelligence would help to bring a hitherto unexampled brilliance to our democracy. But schools alone are not enough; for our habits are in the process of formation in every form of associated activity—in the home and church as well as the school, in all relations of work and play, politics and arts, and in all the means of communication: newspapers, radio, literature, advertising, and so on. Like Mill, Dewey does not think that the native intelligence of the

[u]See Appendix B, p. 118.

average citizen is too limited for effective participation in public life. The rationality required is more a function of acquired habits than innate intellect. If the youth are nurtured in an environment in which democratic/scientific procedures are incarnate, they will acquire the corresponding habits as a matter of course. If they participate in the shared activities of democracy as a way of life, the requisite moral qualities will develop as a natural function of life experience.

> The level of intelligence fixed by *embodied* intelligence is always the important thing. . . . A mechanic can discourse of ohms and amperes as Sir Isaac Newton could not in his day. Many a man who has tinkered with radios can judge of things which Faraday did not dream of. It is aside from the point to say that if Newton and Faraday were here now, the amateur and mechanic would be infants beside them. The retort only brings out the point: the difference made by different objects to think of and by different meanings in circulation. A more intelligent state of social affairs, one more informed with knowledge, more directed by intelligence, would not improve original endowments one whit, but it would raise the level upon which the intelligence of all operates. The height of this level is much more important for judgment of public concerns than are differences in intelligence quotients. (Dewey, 1927, pp. 366–67)[v]

Not only must participants in democratic discourse know how to be experimental, they must also have pertinent scientific information. Scientists, especially social scientists, would play a vital role in social intelligence. They must inform the public concerning the nature of the problematic situations addressed in public policy debates, and they must indicate courses of action that would seem to reconstruct the situation. Economists, for example, must advise the public concerning causes of inflation, unemployment, low productivity, and suchlike; and they must indicate courses of action that would relieve such distresses and improve the economy.

Dewey is aware that professional inquiries are rather dry and dull to the general public. Indeed, he recognizes apathy as one of the chief problems in contemporary politics, and he knows that the typical reports of social scientists might make matters worse. He thinks that apathy about public policy might be significantly reduced if the inquiries of science were directed specifically to matters of concern to private citizens. For example, modern industrial life has disabled and dismembered precious immediate communities to an unprecedented

[v]See Appendix B, p. 142.

degree. Social science would become interesting if its practitioners got away from their abstractions and explained how it has been that community life has been pulverized in this way. They would generate further interest if they suggested hypotheses for social reconstruction that would restore the values of shared experience. When scientific knowledge is shown to have a direct bearing on vital human concerns, it might be enthusiastically sought for. At the same time, in the context of face-to-face communities citizens might feel the intimate importance of policy alternatives; so their discussions of them would be concerned and lively.

> There is no limit to the liberal expansion and confirmation of limited personal intellectual endowment which may proceed from the flow of social intelligence when that circulates by word of mouth from one to another in the communications of the local community. That and that only gives reality to public opinion. We lie, as Emerson said, in the lap of an immense intelligence. But that intelligence is dormant and its communications are broken, inarticulate and faint until it possesses the local community as its medium. (Dewey, 1927, pp. 371–72)[w]

For that matter, scientific information need not be communicated by scientists. Dewey thinks it would be reasonable for journalists to abandon their lust for sensations and scandals and devote themselves instead to communicating the import of social knowledge for the public interest. He even dares hope that individuals with literary and artistic talent might occasionally utilize such gifts for educational purposes. Needless to say, education is distinguished from indoctrination and special pleading, and Dewey ardently hopes that educators and journalists would respect that distinction.

It is noteworthy that Dewey acknowledges that America enjoys much freedom. Nevertheless, he judges our level of public discourse to be low. It is intemperate, inaccurate, incomplete, and deliberately biased; and rather few persons heed it, much less participate in it. He takes this condition to illustrate that freedom of speech in itself is not sufficient to create the elusive morale of constructive public discourse. We must also have the various instruments that are needed to make that freedom effective. Our schools and homes, the practices of daily life, the social sciences, and our media of communication might be modified in a manner to convert an ill-prepared, bewildered, and apathetic mass into a community alive with intelligence. A bold and ambitious vision!

[w]See Appendix B, p. 144.

Dewey's theory of social intelligence is not thoroughly worked out. It is never presented systematically, as I have done it here; and its meaning as a way of life is not elaborated at some crucial junctures. Dewey repeats his advice that all phases of life should be directed by social intelligence, but he does not explain just what this would mean. How is a family, for example, governed by social intelligence? Or education? Business? The military? He does not have in mind that such organizations are to be managed by the ballot, but he certainly advocates that there be consultation, communication, and creative inquiry. In such procedures, what is to be the role of authority—of parent, teacher, owner, executive, and so forth? It is by no means obvious that all groups should make uniform use of social intelligence. Generals might discourse among themselves, but it is not likely that the army could function effectively as a democracy. It is not clear either that the democratization of all phases of life would make people more democratic. It might well be, for example, that strong (and loving) parental authority is essential for the growth of children into secure, responsible, and autonomous adults.

The fact that there are unanswered questions and problematic hypotheses should not be dismaying. There is no greater champion than Dewey of continuing inquiry and revision of belief as evidence requires. Moreover, the issues raised here are not threatening to his basic conception of social intelligence as the means for carrying on the discourse of our public life. Here Dewey displays, I think, an unrivaled wisdom. Of course we should continue to reexamine his assumptions and arguments, and we should consider revised or alternative means for contending with our characteristic predicaments. My belief is that we shall gain more by refining and building upon Dewey than by trying to overturn him.

Although he suggests many reforms for the revitalization of public life, Dewey has less to say about how such reforms might be instituted. In a free and pluralistic society, one can only participate in public discourse, not dictate to it. Rather few of Dewey's ideas have been put into practice. An experimentalist must acknowledge that these proposals are hypothetical. We can make no claim to have confirmation of their efficacy until such time as they would actually be incorporated into our national life. Even so, we have partial evidence for the worth of his ideas in the experience of smaller groups. It is possible to make some judgments about Dewey's philosophy, and Mill's as well. This is the topic of the concluding chapter.

CHAPTER 6

The Challenge from Mill and Dewey

Analysis of these two philosophers shows that they had more about which to agree than to disagree. Both were truly devoted to the liberation and flourishing of human nature. They shared a vision of a free society, governed by the intelligence and virtue of its citizens. They did not think of popular government as a passive recording of antecedently fixed preferences, but as an active process of creating agreement in the ongoing affairs of public life. Communication is the most vital and crucial part of the process. Impartial and intelligent discourse tends, they agreed, to be progressive, self-corrective; but it has no final terminus. Not only will history provide no end of novel predicaments, but the individuals involved in social deliberation will not find perfect agreement.

Both men had very high standards for communication. They deeply regretted sloth, fear and timidity, deceit, complacency, sophistry, dogmatism, and premature conclusions. They equally disliked any mode of argument that resorted to prejudicial attacks on other positions or on their defenders. The love of honest inquiry thrived in Mill and Dewey as it has in few others; and they did not possess the arrogance that would lead them to isolate their thinking from any possible source of help. They loved dialogue, not monologue.

Although Dewey was frequently complimentary to his predecessor, Mill might complain that he received insufficient recognition for his then-radical explorations of the social nature of knowledge and moral evaluation, and for his recognition that intelligence can prosper only in a social medium. We can be confident, on the other hand, that Mill would not hesitate to change his views whenever he found Dewey's alternatives to be cogent.

There are significant differences. Above all, Dewey found Mill's philosophic ideas about human nature and experience to be unequal to the demands made upon them. Associationist psychology gives no clue to the connection between experience and nature, and it is impotent to account for human behavior. Its particular conception of the nature of ideas blinded Mill to the role of hypotheses in inquiry and prevented him from seeing that ideas are prescriptions for the deliberate reconstruction of ongoing events.

Dewey was critical of Mill for his assumption of a presocial human nature. Mill's associationism, however, implies great plasticity in human nature. Indeed, it implies the omnipotence of culture; and on this point Dewey might have more appropriately argued that Mill neglects native biological tendencies. It is clear in any case that the philosophy of education growing out of Mill's associationism is at considerable variance with Dewey's educational theory. In accord with his own philosophy of experience, Dewey believed that we acquire both our moral and intellectual virtues more through overt activity than formal instruction. Mill believed that he was directly taught to be rational and moral. Dewey believed that one learns such things primarily by engaging in activity with other people.

But Mill's philosophical anthropology has an incoherence that neither Mill nor Dewey was aware of. Unreflectively, he was a Lockean individualist. He habitually made reference to human faculties as if they are ready-made powers, needing only to be free of restraint in order to become fully actual by means of their inherent resources. This assumption informs many writings, including *On Liberty*. Accordingly, Mill took the position of Locke and classical liberalism that excellence in public discourse requires only liberty. Insofar as this is indeed Mill's conclusion, he is subject to Dewey's critique of Locke. (So Dewey's complaint of Mill's individualism turned out, accidentally, to be appropriate.) However, the other side of Mill, his associationist side, thought we needed to be educated in a deliberate way to form desirable human qualities.

It may well be that neither of Mill's philosophies of education is adequate. Associationism is surely dead.[1] Lockeanism of a sort may have some life in it, if we think of it as a debate about the existence of native biological conditions that determine fairly definite forms of behavior. This position is distinguishable from Dewey's. Dewey denied that native propensities can by themselves determine a form of action. Many psychologists and sociobiologists, on the other hand, believe otherwise. The nativist view does not constitute a denial, however, that much of the learning process is facilitated and enriched by overt activity. Although native tendencies may be more determinative than Dewey believed, the weight of current evidence is largely supportive of his view that interpersonal relations make a decisive difference in the formation of moral traits.

In the spirit of Mill and Dewey, we cannot consider the inquiry into human nature and education to be closed. Accordingly, we can by no means speak with finality about what sort of educational institutions would engender the excellence in our public debates that Mill and Dewey hoped for. At this point it will be helpful to examine their philosophical similarities more closely.

Mill's *Liberty* is justly studied for its presentation of a principle defining the limits of authority over the individual. It is justly celebrated for its defense of freedom of speech, and it is justly admired for its analysis and defense of human individuality. I trust that some of the preceding discussions have shown that there is still more in that little volume. It contains considerably more of an idea of social intelligence than has typically been recognized. For this reason (as well as others) I think it is not presumptuous to assume that Mill would be sympathetic to Dewey's more elaborate development of the notion. My principal reservation about this assumption concerns the status of Mill's utilitarianism. One cannot be sure whether the fallibilism expressed in *Liberty* is meant to extend to the idea that utility is to be regarded as the exclusive test of morality. If fallibilism applies to the principle of utility (as it should), then Mill would seem to belong fully and forthrightly to the philosophy of social intelligence. He consistently regards himself as a utilitarian, however.

Perhaps his exclusive allegiance to utility has more to do with historical context than anything else. He saw it as directed impartially to human emancipation and fulfillment, and these were clearly what he desired at bottom. The alternative ethical theories known to him seemed incoherent or reactionary. Hence utilitarianism seemed obviously correct. It is significant that he struggled with it so deeply that he eradicated the strictly Benthamite version of it in his own theory. It was hardly recognizable any more as utilitarianism. All this being so, it is not difficult to believe that with more systematic thinking Mill might have embraced social intelligence in an unqualified way.

One of the distinctive characteristics of social intelligence is that it does not presuppose any unconditional moral values. Many thinkers are supportive of democracy, but they assume that it must be justified on some definite moral foundation, such as utility, natural rights, or a social contract. As far as Dewey—if not Mill—is concerned, however, democracy presupposes an irreducible plurality of values, no one of which can be regarded as invariably decisive. In their quest for certainty, philosophers might find this embarrassing; but pluralism can well be regarded as an asset. Democracy is the attempt to serve and fulfill the moral life more amply than any alternative, and social intelligence is its method. To be sure, social intelligence presupposes a kind of moral equality, or impartiality; but this equality does not entail specific rights and duties. It does not by itself solve moral dilemmas. I might have equal respect for your values and for those of someone with whom you disagree. Perhaps you are concerned uppermost with utility in the case at issue, while she regards rights as of greatest concern. My impartiality does not make any situation easier; it makes it more difficult.

Conscientious moral disagreement is one of the most conspicuous phenomena of the moral life. If it did not occur, there would not be occasion for moral philosophy. Philosophers react to it either by throwing up their hands in despair or by attempting to succeed where all others have failed: to reduce plurality to unity. (One must admire them, I suppose, for their Sisyphean persistence.) If we disdain to remove moral disagreement by force or by thought control, then social intelligence presents itself as the most effective means so far contrived for carrying on the moral life. If one appreciates the virtues of social intelligence, he will also have the deepest possible understanding of the importance of excellence in public discourse.

For the moral absolutist, such discourse is a sort of luxury. After all, if you know what is good independently of communication, there is no particular imperative to indulge in it. I commented a moment ago that many philosophers defend democracy, but they do so by looking for an undergirding absolute. There is a kind of paradox in that position. In the terms of that argument, the undergirding must be thought of as taking precedence over what it supports. Accordingly, democracy can be limited or sacrificed in deference to what underlies it. In Rawls's theory, for example, the principles of justice provide for a democracy of sorts, but a democratic public can never disqualify or even so much as modify those principles. The democracy of Dewey, and Mill in some moments, is more radical, and the quality of its discourse is more crucial.

Bear in mind that this is not a democracy equated with majority rule. Majorities have perpetrated all manner of misdeeds. Social intelligence is not a morally neutral operation. It presupposes a kind of moral equality, and it demands a certain arsenal of moral and intellectual excellences. Consider some of the importance of these virtues. The parties subscribing to the method do not think of themselves as engaged in an intransigent power struggle. They are not bent on exploiting one another. Ideally, they would have genuine regard for one another and would wish to be mutually supportive and to share in common activities. At the least, they would be tolerant and have mutual respect.

It is difficult to underrate the importance of the obviously scientific elements in the democratic morale. As a matter of fact, most controversies are conducted with little regard for inquiry. A few impressions, a few slogans, some propaganda—combined with overheated passions—suffice to give permanent definition to one's stance in a dispute. Many of the public policy debates in America today are not reducible to strictly moral issues, but hinge decisively on disputes about the facts. We struggle about the danger of nuclear power plants, for example, or we contest the feasibility of the Strategic Defense Initiative/"Star Wars" project. The greatest single consideration dividing factions in both foreign policy and defense issues is whether the Soviet Union is an inherently imperialist power or whether its behavior is a defensive reaction to United States policy. All these are questions of fact. The factual question alone does not decide problematic policy, but often it does turn out to be the crucial item in contention. Unscientific people—including many scientists—already have their minds made up about these torments, and they have no wish to hear any other side of the matter. The problem is greatly compounded when those responsible for investigating and reporting the facts cannot be trusted. Where does one go for help?

If people do not wish to tamper with their convictions about questions of fact, still less do they wish to consider new alternatives or share in their formulation. They prefer to adopt the same loyalty to their beliefs that might be reserved for the local baseball team or a family heirloom. Stick to them win or lose, beautiful or ugly, no matter what! That is fine for home-team partisanship and family heirlooms; but Mill and Dewey want us to realize that it is a misplaced allegiance to hold on to ideas in the same manner. It is also self-defeating. If situations are to be converted from problematic to consummatory, there is no substitute for knowing what is really happening. The method of the ostrich is not recommended.

The merits of the open mind seem obvious. Somehow, however, we are too lazy, jealous, defensive, or timid to want to engage in serious inquiry. The problem is intensified when not just the facts, but our moral convictions are at issue. Mill and Dewey were well aware of this. Mill believed, in effect, that peer pressure is the greatest obstacle to intellectual honesty and freedom. Dewey tended to think it is habituated complacency in the face of authority. Neither one believed it is a genetic limitation; but it can hardly be doubted that a change in our habits is very difficult to accomplish.

Social intelligence makes great demands on its participants. We must not suffer from an obsessive demand that other people conform to our antecedently given wishes. We must be willing to engage in cooperative communication and to be flexible in our planning. These are rare, but precious, talents for both the happiness of their possessor and the welfare of society. At the same time, social intelligence incorporates many traditional virtues. Surely courage, for example, is required to resist the demand for conformity or to be willing to argue with abusive individuals. It is equally required in taking a moral stand. Neither Mill nor Dewey was an advocate of caving in to the majority. The reasonable inquiries of a moral situation might well lead one to an unpopular decision.

Despite the differences in their respective theories of human nature, Mill and Dewey agreed that virtually everyone can somehow be raised to a level of competence, if not excellence, as participants in democratic life. It is a hopeful thought; but both might well be wrong in such a sweeping claim. It would be a disastrous error, however, to dismiss Mill and Dewey if both of them are mistaken in their optimism. Perhaps a certain percentage of the population lacks the native ability ever to be effective participants in social intelligence. Another percentage will be more or less marginal regarding their capacity, and hence movable by education in one direction or the other. Another group will be capable of a significant measure of informed and rational discussion.

If some division of this sort is realistic, it still behooves us on grounds of both self-interest and regard for others to seek ways to educate everyone to the limits of their capacity. It likewise behooves us that their interests be consulted regarding issues of public policy. Only then can anyone learn "where the shoe pinches"; and only under conditions of genuine consultation would such persons be treated with respect. Whatever possibilities for intelligent participation one has, they will not be cultivated if they are rejected out of hand. What would be the point of systematically excluding any group from participation in public discourse? That is the sort of thing done by dictators, and they do it to consolidate their power. In any society, those excluded from participation are those most eligible to be exploited.

Of course there is a very large, if indeterminate, number of persons who might function much as Mill and Dewey recommended. It is also safe to conclude that much the greater part of these is functioning well below that standard. This does not seem to be a problem of native capacity, but of education. I offered the opinion in the introduction that public discourse in America is much deteriorated. Intellectuals, professors, journalists, media pundits, religious leaders, and the "politically sophisticated" public seem to be moving steadily in the direction of dogmatism, intolerance, anger, and recrimination. If their behavior falls so short of excellence, they have little justification to complain of the quality of the democratic public. When teachers and professors, for example, display no respect for academic freedom, dissent, and conscientious inquiry into the realities of public affairs, what must our students learn from such a display? Too many of them are persuaded that pompous moral indignation is somehow more admirable than patient analysis. The closed mind supersedes the spirit of cooperative inquiry.

It is hard to believe that a phenomenon of this sort is due to deficient intelligence or a constitutional necessity to be intemperate. Many of the perpetrators are extremely intelligent, and I presume their emotions are not altogether out of their control. The causes of the maladies in our discourse are no doubt diverse and lie far afield. They are a matter for serious investigation. One may insist, however, that our ailments are largely remediable. One may be confident of such a conclusion just because it is clear that there are variations of better and worse in the behavior of every person. Likewise, there are people, like Mill and Dewey themselves, who are rather good at social intelligence. But persons of a comparable natural endowment can behave like juveniles. What makes the difference? Whatever it is, it is a problem of education, broadly conceived.

Social intelligence is a process carried on by mortal flesh, not by philosophical inventions. For this reason its discourse will always be flawed, and its conclusions not uniformly acceptable. Although we cannot be sure just what the inherent limitations and resources of human nature are, we have enough historical experience to believe that the instruments devised by Mill and Dewey are somewhere within our competence. Even if we cannot master them as well as these authors hoped, they are still our best resource for contending with the characteristic problems of associated life.

APPENDIXES

NOTES

REFERENCES

FURTHER SCHOLARLY
RESOURCES

INDEX

ABOUT THE AUTHOR

John Stuart Mill

Excerpt from *On Liberty*

In chapter I of *On Liberty* Mill advances a principle of liberty that defines the limits of rightful encroachment by government or society on the freedom of the individual. The meaning and application of the principle are not as clear as Mill supposed; nor is its relationship to the principle of utility obvious.[1] The argument below, however, which is chapter II of *On Liberty*, does not invoke the principle enunciated in the first chapter. Freedom of speech is defended because of its highly desirable consequences for both the individual and society. The selection omits Mill's footnotes, and it omits those passages that are simply illustrative or are comments on conditions in England at the time of Mill's writing.

While there have been various interpretations of Mill's argument and many criticisms of it, no systematic writing has come forth to replace it. It remains an extremely powerful and influential defense of the liberty on which excellence in public discourse depends.

"OF THE LIBERTY OF THOUGHT AND DISCUSSION"

Mill begins by arguing that no government may rightly prescribe opinions to its citizens, nor proscribe them either. Indeed, no majority, however large, may rightly silence any minority, no matter how small. The first

reason that Mill gives for this assertion is that such limitations block the
search for truth. Anyone who would obstruct inquiry and criticism assumes
his own infallibility—at least in the sense that he would withhold from others
the conditions necessary to determine the truth.

The time, it is hoped, is gone by when any defense would be necessary of the "liberty of the press" as one of the securities against corrupt or tyrannical government. No argument, we may suppose, can
now be needed against permitting a legislature or an executive, not
identified in interest with the people, to prescribe opinions to them
and determine what doctrines or what arguments they shall be allowed to hear. This aspect of the question, besides, has been so often
and so triumphantly enforced by preceding writers that it needs not be
specially insisted on in this place. Though the law of England, on the
subject of the press, is as servile to this day as it was in the time of the
Tudors, there is little danger of its being actually put in force against
political discussion except during some temporary panic when fear of
insurrection drives ministers and judges from their propriety; and,
speaking generally, it is not, in constitutional countries, to be ap-
prehended that the government, whether completely responsible to
the people or not, will often attempt to control the expression of opinion, except when in doing so it makes itself the organ of the general
intolerance of the public. Let us suppose, therefore, that the government is entirely at one with the people, and never thinks of exerting
any power of coercion unless in agreement with what it conceives to
be their voice. But I deny the right of the people to exercise such coercion, either by themselves or by their government. The power itself is
illegitimate. The best government has no more title to it than the
worst. It is as noxious, or more noxious, when exerted in accordance
with public opinion than when in opposition to it. If all mankind
minus one were of one opinion, mankind would be no more justified
in silencing that one person than he, if he had the power, would be
justified in silencing mankind. Were an opinion a personal possession of no value except to the owner, if to be obstructed in the enjoyment of it were simply a private injury, it would make some difference whether the injury was inflicted only on a few persons or on
many. But the peculiar evil of silencing the expression of an opinion
is that it is robbing the human race, posterity as well as the existing
generation—those who dissent from the opinion, still more than
those who hold it. If the opinion is right, they are deprived of the opportunity of exchanging error for truth; if wrong, they lose, what is

almost as great a benefit, the clearer perception and livelier impression of truth produced by its collision with error.

It is necessary to consider separately these two hypotheses, each of which has a distinct branch of the argument corresponding to it. We can never be sure that the opinion we are endeavoring to stifle is a false opinion; and if we were sure, stifling it would be an evil still.

First, the opinion which it is attempted to suppress by authority may possibly be true. Those who desire to suppress it, of course, deny its truth; but they are not infallible. They have no authority to decide the question for all mankind and exclude every other person from the means of judging. To refuse a hearing to an opinion because they are sure that it is false is to assume that *their* certainty is the same thing as *absolute* certainty. All silencing of discussion is an assumption of infallibility. Its condemnation may be allowed to rest on this common argument, not the worse for being common.

Unfortunately for the good sense of mankind, the fact of their fallibility is far from carrying the weight in their practical judgment which is always allowed to it in theory; for while everyone well knows himself to be fallible, few think it necessary to take any precautions against their own fallibility, or admit the supposition that any opinion of which they feel very certain may be one of the examples of the error to which they acknowledge themselves to be liable. Absolute princes, or others who are accustomed to unlimited deference, usually feel this complete confidence in their own opinions on nearly all subjects. People more happily situated, who sometimes hear their opinions disputed and are not wholly unused to be set right when they are wrong, place the same unbounded reliance only on such of their opinions as are shared by all who surround them, or to whom they habitually defer; for in proportion to a man's want of confidence in his own solitary judgment does he usually repose, with implicit trust, on the infallibility of "the world" in general. And the world, to each individual, means the part of it with which he comes in contact: his party, his sect, his church, his class of society; the man may be called, by comparison, almost liberal and large-minded to whom it means anything so comprehensive as his own country or his own age. Nor is his faith in this collective authority at all shaken by his being aware that other ages, countries, sects, churches, classes, and parties have thought, and even now think, the exact reverse. He devolves upon his own world the responsibility of being in the right against the dissentient worlds of other people; and it never troubles him that mere accident has decided which of these numerous worlds is the object of his reliance, and that the same causes which make him a churchman in London would have made him a Buddhist or a Confucian in Peking. Yet it is as evident in itself, as any amount of argument can make, that ages are no more infallible than individuals—every age having held many opinions which subsequent ages have deemed not only false but absurd; and it is as certain that many opinions, now general, will be rejected by future ages, as it is that many, once general, are rejected by the present.

The objection likely to be made to this argument would probably take some such form as the following. There is no greater assumption of infallibility in forbidding the propagation of error than in any other thing which is done by public authority on its own judgment and responsibility. Judgment is given to men that they may use it. Because it may be used erroneously, are men to be told that they ought not to use it at all? To prohibit what they think pernicious is not claiming exemption from error, but fulfilling the duty incumbent on them, although fallible, of acting on their conscientious conviction. If we were never to act on our opinions, because those opinions may be wrong, we should leave all our interests uncared for, and all our duties unperformed. An objection which applies to all conduct can be no valid objection to any conduct in particular. It is the duty of governments, and of individuals, to form the truest opinions they can; to form them carefully, and never impose them upon others unless they are quite sure of being right. But when they are sure (such reasoners may say), it is not conscientiousness but cowardice to shrink from acting on their opinions and allow doctrines which they honestly think dangerous to the welfare of mankind, either in this life or in another, to be scattered abroad without restraint, because other people, in less enlightened times, have persecuted opinions now believed to be true. Let us take care, it may be said, not to make the same mistake; but governments and nations have made mistakes in other things which are not denied to be fit subjects for the exercise of authority: they have laid on bad taxes, made unjust wars. Ought we therefore to lay on no taxes and, under whatever provocation, make no wars? Men and governments must act to the best of their ability. There is no such thing as absolute certainty, but there is assurance sufficient for the purposes of human life. We may, and must, assume our opinion to be true for the guidance of our own conduct; and it is assuming no more when we forbid bad men to pervert society by the propagation of opinions which we regard as false and pernicious.

I answer, that it is assuming very much more. There is the greatest difference between presuming an opinion to be true because, with every opportunity for contesting it, it has not been refuted, and assuming its truth for the purpose of not permitting its refutation. Complete liberty of contradicting and disproving our opinion is the very condition which justifies us in assuming its truth for purposes of action; and on no other terms can a being with human faculties have any rational assurance of being right.

Mill's emphasis is on criticising *opinions; and his analysis is insofar limited. He does not possess a conception of ideas as working hypotheses for innovative action. His insistence that ideas can be adequately tested only by subjecting them to unlimited examination by other persons is, however, a new and profoundly important idea. The principal remedy for the limitations of the individual mind is participation in a process of criticism.*

Mill does not distinguish in this essay between moral and scientific arguments; so he does not indicate in what ways the two types of argument might differ. It is clear, however, that he believes that any kind of rational confidence in an argument must be predicated on its being open to all comers. In this fundamental sense, moral and scientific discourse are the same. Hence Mill is a great critic of individualism not only in science, but in moral deliberation as well.

When we consider either the history of opinion or the ordinary conduct of human life, to what is it to be ascribed that the one and the other are no worse than they are? Not certainly to the inherent force of the human understanding, for on any matter not self-evident there are ninety-nine persons totally incapable of judging of it for one who is capable; and the capacity of the hundredth person is only comparative, for the majority of the eminent men of every past generation held many opinions now known to be erroneous, and did or approved numerous things which no one will now justify. Why is it, then, that there is on the whole a preponderance among mankind of rational opinions and rational conduct? If there really is this preponderance—which there must be unless human affairs are, and have always been, in an almost desperate state—it is owing to a quality of the human mind, the source of everything respectable in man either as an intellectual or as a moral being, namely, that his errors are corrigible. He is capable of rectifying his mistakes by discussion and experience. Not by experience alone. There must be discussion to show how experience is to be interpreted. Wrong opinions and practices gradually yield to fact and argument; but facts and arguments, to produce any effect on the mind, must be brought before it. Very few facts are able to tell their own story, without comments to bring out their meaning. The whole strength and value, then, of human judgment depending on the one property, that it can be set right when it is wrong, reliance can be placed on it only when the means of setting it right are kept constantly at hand. In the case of any person whose judgment is really deserving of confidence, how has it become so? Because he has kept his mind open to criticism of his opinions and conduct. Because it has been his practice to listen to all that could be said against him; to profit by as much of it as was just, and to expound to himself, and upon occasion to others, the fallacy of what was fallacious. Because he has felt that the only way in which a human being can make some approach to knowing the whole of a subject is by hearing what can be said about it by persons of every variety of opinion, and studying all modes, in which it can be looked at by every character of mind. No wise man ever acquired his wisdom in any mode but this; nor is it in the nature of human intellect to become wise in any other manner. The steady habit of correcting and completing his own opinion by collating it with those of others, so far from causing doubt and hesitation in carrying it into practice, is the only stable foundation for a just reliance on it; for, being cognizant of all that can, at least obviously, be said against him, and having taken up his position against all gainsayers—knowing that he has sought for objections and difficulties instead of avoiding them, and has shut out no light which can be thrown upon the subject from any quarter—he has a right to think his judgment better than that of any person, or any multitude, who have not gone through a similar process.

It is not too much to require that what the wisest of mankind, those who are best entitled to trust their own judgment, find necessary to warrant their relying on it, should be submitted to by that miscellaneous collection of a few wise and many foolish individuals called the public. The most intolerant of churches, the Roman Catholic Church, even at the canonization of a saint admits, and listens patiently to, a "devil's advocate." The holiest of men, it appears, cannot be admitted to posthumous honors until all that the devil could say against him is known and weighed. If even the Newtonian philosophy were not permitted to be questioned, mankind could not feel as complete assurance of its truth as they now do. The beliefs which we have most warrant for have no safeguard to rest on but a standing invitation to the whole world to prove them unfounded. If the challenge is not accepted, or is accepted and the attempt fails, we are far enough from certainty still, but we have done the best that the existing state of human reason admits of: we have neglected nothing that could give the truth a chance of reaching us;

if the lists are kept open, we may hope that, if there be a better truth, it will be found when the human mind is capable of receiving it; and in the meantime we may rely on having attained such approach to truth as is possible in our own day. This is the amount of certainty attainable by a fallible being, and this the sole way of attaining it.

Strange it is that men should admit the validity of the arguments for free discussion, but object to their being "pushed to an extreme," not seeing that unless the reasons are good for an extreme case, they are not good for any case. Strange that they should imagine that they are not assuming infallibility when they acknowledge that there should be free discussion on all subjects which can possibly be *doubtful,* but think that some particular principle or doctrine should be forbidden to be questioned because it is so *certain,* that is, because *they are certain* that it is certain. To call any proposition certain while there is anyone who would deny its certainty if permitted, but who is not permitted, is to assume that we ourselves, and those who agree with us, are the judges of certainty, and judges without hearing the other side.

In the present age—which has been described as "destitute of faith, but terrified at skepticism"—in which people feel sure, not so much that their opinions are true as that they should not know what to do with them—the claims of an opinion to be protected from public attack are rested not so much on its truth as on its importance to society. There are, it is alleged, certain beliefs so useful, not to say indispensable, to well-being that it is as much the duty of governments to uphold those beliefs as to protect any other of the interests of society. In a case of such necessity, and so directly in the line of their duty, something less than infallibility may, it is maintained, warrant, and even bind, governments to act on their own opinion confirmed by the general opinion of mankind. It is also often argued, and still oftener thought, that none but bad men would desire to weaken these salutary beliefs; and there can be nothing wrong, it is thought, in restraining bad men and prohibiting what only such men would wish to practice. This mode of thinking makes the justification of restraints on discussion not a question of the truth of doctrines but of their usefulness, and flatters itself by that means to escape the responsibility of claiming to be an infallible judge of opinions. But those who thus satisfy themselves do not perceive that the assumption of infallibility is merely shifted from one point to another. The usefulness of an opinion is itself matter of opinion—as disputable, as open to discussion, and requiring discussion as much as the opinion itself. There is the same need of an infallible judge of opinions to decide an opinion

to be noxious as to decide it to be false, unless the opinion condemned has full opportunity of defending itself. And it will not do to
say that the heretic may be allowed to maintain the utility or harm-
lessness of his opinion, though forbidden to maintain its truth. The
truth of an opinion is part of its utility. If we would know whether or
not it is desirable that a proposition should be believed, is it possible
to exclude the consideration of whether or not it is true? In the opinion, not of bad men, but of the best men, no belief which is contrary
to truth can be really useful; and can you prevent such men from urging that plea when they are charged with culpability for denying
some doctrine which they are told is useful, but which they believe to
be false? Those who are on the side of received opinions never fail to
take all possible advantage of this plea; you do not find *them* handling
the question of ability as if it could be completely abstracted from that
of truth; on the contrary, it is, above all, because their doctrine is "the
truth" that the knowledge or the belief of it is held to be so indispensable. There can be no fair discussion of the question of usefulness
when an argument so vital may be employed on one side, but not on
the other. And in point of fact, when law or public feeling do not permit the truth of an opinion to be disputed, they are just as little
tolerant of a denial of its usefulness. The utmost they allow is an
extenuation of its absolute necessity, or of the positive guilt of re-
jecting it.

In order more fully to illustrate the mischief of denying a hearing
to opinions because we, in our own judgment, have condemned
them, it will be desirable to fix down the discussion to a concrete case;
and I choose, by preference, the cases which are least favorable to
me—in which the argument against freedom of opinion, both on the
score of truth and on that of utility, is considered the strongest. Let
the opinions impugned be the belief in a God and in a future state, or
any of the commonly received doctrines of morality. To fight the
battle on such ground gives a great advantage to an unfair antagonist,
since he will be sure to say (and many who have no desire to be unfair
will say it internally), Are these the doctrines which you do not deem
sufficiently certain to be taken under the protection of law? Is the
belief in a God one of the opinions to feel sure of which you hold to
be assuming infallibility? But I must be permitted to observe that it is
not the feeling sure of a doctrine (be it what it may) which I call an
assumption of infalliblity. It is the undertaking to decide that question
for others, without allowing them to hear what can be said on the contrary side. And I denounce and reprobate this pretension not the less
if put forth on the side of my most solemn convictions. However

positive anyone's persuasion may be, not only of the falsity but of the pernicious consequences—not only of the pernicious consequences, but (to adopt expressions which I altogether condemn) the immorality and impiety of an opinion—yet if, in pursuance of that private judgment, though backed by the public judgment of his country or his contemporaries, he prevents the opinion from being heard in its defense, he assumes infallibility. And so far from the assumption being less objectionable or less dangerous because the opinion is called immoral or impious, this is the case of all others in which it is most fatal. These are exactly the occasions on which the men of one generation commit those dreadful mistakes which excite the astonishment and horror of posterity. It is among such that we find the instances memorable in history, when the arm of the law has been employed to root out the best men and the noblest doctrines; with deplorable success as to the men, though some of the doctrines have survived to be (as if in mockery) invoked in defense of similar conduct toward those who dissent from *them*, or from their received interpretation.

In the persecution of such persons as Socrates and Jesus, there is dramatic verification of Mill's contention that the ideas prohibited in a society might turn out to be extremely beneficial. The persecution of Christians by Marcus Aurelius shows that intolerance is not necessarily the result of malice or stupidity. This particular Roman emperor was a person of great intelligence and virtue; but he was not infallible. Mill's arguments against censorship and intimidation do not apply just to the ignorant and wicked; and one may not assume that he has the authority to decide what shall be written and spoken just because he has benevolent motives.

Mankind can hardly be too often reminded that there was once a man called Socrates, between whom and the legal authorities and public opinion of his time there took place a memorable collision. Born in an age and country abounding in individual greatness, this man has been handed down to us by those who best knew both him and the age as the most virtuous man in it; while *we* know him as the head and prototype of all subsequent teachers of virtue, the source equally of the lofty inspiration of Plato and the judicious utilitarianism of Aristotle, *"i maestri di color che sanno,"* the two headsprings of ethical as of all other philosophy. This acknowledged master of all the eminent thinkers who have since lived—whose fame, still growing after more than two thousand years, all but outweighs the whole remainder of the names which make his native city illustrious—was put to death by his countrymen, after a judicial conviction, for impiety and immorality. Impiety, in denying the gods recognized by the State; indeed, his accuser asserted (see the *Apologia*) that he believed in no gods at all. Immorality, in being, by his doctrines and instructions, a "corruptor of youth." Of these charges the tribunal, there is every ground for believing, honestly found him guilty, and condemned the man who probably of all then born had deserved best of mankind to be put to death as a criminal.

To pass from this to the only other instance of judicial iniquity, the mention of which, after the condemnation of Socrates, would not be an anticlimax: the event which took place on Calvary rather more than eighteen hundred years ago. The man who left on the memory of those who witnessed his life and conversation such as impression of his moral grandeur that eighteen subsequent centuries have done homage to him as the Almighty in person, was ignominiously put to death, as what? As a blasphemer. Men did not merely mistake their benefactor, they mistook him for the exact contrary of what he was and treated him as the prodigy of impiety which they themselves are now held to be for their treatment of him. The feelings with which mankind now regard these lamentable transactions, especially the later of the two, render them extremely unjust in their judgment of the unhappy actors. These were, to all appearance, not bad men—not worse than men commonly are, but rather the contrary; men who possessed in a full, or somewhat more than a full measure, the religious, moral, and patriotic feelings of their time and people: the very kind of men who, in all times, our own included, have every chance of passing through life blameless and respected. The high priest who rent his garments when the words were pronounced, which, according to all the ideas of his country, constituted the blackest guilt, was in all probability quite as sincere in his horror and indignation as the generality of respectable and pious men now are in the religious and moral sentiments they profess; and most of those who now shudder at his conduct, if they had lived in his time, and been born Jews, would have acted precisely as he did. Orthodox Christians who are tempted to think that those who stoned to death the first martyrs must have been worse men than they themselves are ought to remember that one of those persecutors was Saint Paul.

Let us add one more example, the most striking of all, if the impressiveness of an error is measured by the wisdom and virtue of him who falls into it. If ever anyone possessed of power had grounds for thinking himself the best and most enlightened among his contemporaries, it was the Emperor Marcus Aurelius. Absolute monarch of the whole civilized world, he preserved through life not only the most unblemished justice, but what was less to be expected from his Stoical breeding, the tenderest heart. The few failings which are attributed to him were all on the side of indulgence, while his writings, the highest ethical product of the ancient mind, differ scarcely perceptibly, if they differ at all, from the most characteristic teachings of Christ. This man, a better Christian in all but the dogmatic sense of the word than almost any of the ostensibly Christian sovereigns who have since reigned, persecuted Christianity. Placed at the summit of all the previous attainments of humanity, with an open, unfettered intellect, and a character which led him of himself to embody in his moral writings the Christian ideal, he yet failed to see that Christianity was to be a good and not an evil to the world, with his duties to which he was so deeply penetrated. Existing society he knew to be in a deplorable state. But such as it was, he saw, or thought he saw, that it was held together, and prevented from being worse, by belief and reverence of the received divinities. As a ruler of mankind, he deemed it his duty not to suffer society to fall in pieces; and saw not how, if its existing ties were removed, any others could be formed which could again knit it together. The new religion openly aimed at dissolving these ties; unless, therefore, it was his duty to adopt that religion, it seemed to be his duty to put it down. Inasmuch then as the theology of Christianity did not appear to him true or of divine origin, inasmuch as this strange history of a crucified God was not credible to him, and a system which purported to rest entirely upon a foundation to him so wholly unbelievable, could not be foreseen by him to be that renovating agency which, after all abatements, it has in fact proved to be; the gentlest and most amiable of philosophers and rulers, under a solemn sense of duty, authorized the persecution of Christianity. To my mind this is one of the most tragical facts in all history. It is a bitter thought how different a thing the Christianity of the world might have been if the Christian faith had been adopted as the religion of the empire under the auspices of Marcus Aurelius instead of those of Constantine. But it would be equally unjust to him and false to truth to deny that no one plea which can be urged for punishing anti-Christian teaching was wanting to Marcus Aurelius for punishing, as he did, the propagation of Christianity. No Christian more firmly believes that atheism is false and tends to the dissolution of society than Marcus Aurelius believed the same things of Christianity; he who, of all men then living, might have been thought the most capable of appreciating it. Unless anyone who approves of punishment for the promulgation of opinions flatters himself that he is a wiser and better man than Marcus Aurelius—more deeply versed in the wisdom of his time, more elevated in his intellect above it, more earnest in his search for truth, or more single-minded in his devotion to it when found—let him abstain from that assumption of the joint infallibility of himself and the multitude which the great Antoninus [Aurelius] made with so unfortunate a result. . . .

Mill is as concerned for the development of clear, strong intellects as he is for the pursuit of truth; and the basis for both conditions is the same: freedom. Freedom must have more than legal guarantees; it must also be supported by a morale that pervades the entire society. Intolerance of heterodox thinking is injurious not just because of harm done to the thinker. Even when we remember that intolerance of ideas deprives us of knowledge, we still have not surveyed all of the evils of the narrowed or closed mind. We must also realize that a climate of hostility to unpopular opinions will greatly hinder the development of honest and inquiring minds throughout society. If we keep silence out of fear, Mill adds, or if we refuse to consider alternatives to our own beliefs, we will never be entitled to confidence that our beliefs are true. In the absence of freedom, what might be vital conviction becomes stale dogma.

. . . But though we do not now inflict so much evil on those who think differently from us as it was formerly our custom to do, it may be that we do ourselves as much evil as ever by our treatment of them. Socrates was put to death, but the Socratic philosophy rose like the sun in heaven and spread its illumination over the whole intellectual firmament. Christians were cast to the lions, but the Christian church grew up a stately and spreading tree, overtopping the older and less vigorous growths, and stifling them by its shade. Our merely social intolerance kills no one, roots out no opinions, but induces men to disguise them or to abstain from any active effort for their diffusion. With us, heretical opinions do not perceptibly gain, or even lose, ground in each decade or generation; they never blaze out far and wide, but continue to smolder in the narrow circles of thinking and studious persons among whom they originate, without ever lighting up the general affairs of mankind with either a true or a deceptive light. And thus is kept up a state of things very satisfactory to some minds, because, without the unpleasant process of fining or imprisoning anybody, it maintains all prevailing opinions outwardly undisturbed, while it does not absolutely interdict the exercise of reason by dissentients afflicted with the malady of thought. A convenient plan for having peace in the intellectual world, and keeping all things going on therein very much as they do already. But the price paid for this sort of intellectual pacification is the sacrifice of the entire moral courage of the human mind. A state of things in which a large portion of the most active and inquiring intellects find it advisable to keep the general principles and grounds of their convictions within their own breasts, and attempt, in what they address to the public, to fit as much as they can of their own conclusions to premises which they have internally renounced, cannot send forth the open, fearless characters and logical, consistent intellects who once adorned the thinking world. The sort of men who can be looked for under it are either mere conformers to commonplace, or time-servers for truth, whose arguments on all great subjects are meant for their hearers, and are not those which have convinced themselves. Those who avoid this alternative do so by narrowing their thoughts and interest to things which can be spoken of without venturing within the region of principles, that is, to small practical matters which would come right of themselves, if but the minds of mankind were strengthened and enlarged, and which will never be made effectually right until then, while that which would strengthen and enlarge men's minds—free and daring speculation on the highest subjects—is abandoned.

Those in whose eyes this reticence on the part of heretics is no evil should consider, in the first place, that in consequence of it there is never any fair and thorough discussion of heretical opinions; and that such of them as could not stand such a discussion, though they may be prevented from spreading, do not disappear. But it is not the minds of heretics that are deteriorated most by the ban placed on all inquiry which does not end in the orthodox conclusions. The greatest harm done is to those who are not heretics, and whose whole mental development is cramped and their reason cowed by the fear of heresy. Who can compute what the world loses in the multitude of promising intellects combined with timid characters, who dare not follow out any bold, vigorous, independent train of thought, lest it should land them in something which would admit of being considered irreligious or immoral? Among them we may occasionally see some man of deep conscientiousness and subtle and refined understanding, who spends a life in sophisticating with an intellect which he cannot silence, and exhausts the resources of ingenuity in attempting to reconcile the promptings of his conscience and reason with orthodoxy, which yet he does not, perhaps, to the end succeed in doing. No one can be a great thinker who does not recognize that as a thinker it is his first duty to follow his intellect to whatever conclusions it may lead. Truth gains more even by the errors of one who, with due study and preparation, thinks for himself than by the true opinions of those who only hold them because they do not suffer themselves to think. Not that it is solely, or chiefly, to form great thinkers that freedom of thinking is required. On the contrary, it is as much and even more indispensable to enable average human beings to attain the mental stature which they are capable of. There have been, and may again be, great individual thinkers in a general atmosphere of mental slavery. But there never has been, nor ever will be, in that atmosphere an intellectually active people. Where any people has made a temporary approach to such a character, it has been because the dread of heterodox speculation was for a time suspended. Where there is a tacit convention that principles are not to be disputed, where the discussion of the greatest questions which can occupy humanity is considered to be closed, we cannot hope to find that generally high scale of mental activity which has made some periods of history so remarkable. Never when controversy avoided the subjects which are large and important enough to kindle enthusiasm was the mind of a people stirred up from its foundations, and the impulse given which raised even persons of the most ordinary intellect to something of the dignity of thinking beings. Of such we have had an example in the condition of Europe during the times immediately following the Reformation; another, though limited to the Continent and to a more cultivated class, in the speculative movement of the latter half of the eighteenth century; and a third, of still briefer duration, in the intellectual fermentation of Germany during the Goethian and Fichtean period. These periods differed widely in the particular opinions which they developed, but were alike in this, that during all three the yoke of authority was broken. In each, an old mental despotism had been thrown off, and no new one had yet taken its place. The impulse given at these three periods has made Europe what it now is. Every single improvement which has taken place either in the human mind or in institutions may be traced distinctly to one or other of them. Appearances have for some time indicated that all three impulses are well-nigh spent; and we can expect no fresh start until we again assert our mental freedom.

Let us now pass to the second division of the argument, and dismissing the supposition that any of the received opinions may be false, let us assume them to be true and examine into the worth of the manner in which they are likely to be held when their truth is not freely and openly canvassed. However unwillingly a person who has a strong opinion may admit the possibility that his opinion may be false, he ought to be moved by the consideration that, however true it may be, if it is not fully, frequently, and fearlessly discussed, it will be held as a dead dogma, not a living truth.

There is a class of persons (happily not quite so numerous as formerly) who think it enough if a person assents undoubtingly to what they think true, though he has no knowledge whatever of the grounds of the opinion and could not make a tenable defense of it against the most superficial objections. Such persons, if they can once get their creed taught from authority, naturally think that no good, and some harm, comes of its being allowed to be questioned. Where their influence prevails, they make it nearly impossible for the received opinion to be rejected wisely and considerately, though it may still be rejected rashly and ignorantly; for to shut out discussion entirely is seldom possible, and when it once gets in, beliefs not grounded on conviction are apt to give way before the slightest semblance of an argument. Waiving, however, this possibility—assuming that the true opinion abides in the mind, but abides as a prejudice, a belief independent of, and proof against, argument—this is not the way in which truth ought to be held by a rational being. This is not knowing the truth. Truth, thus held, is but one superstition the more, accidentally clinging to the words which enunciate a truth.

If the intellect and judgment of mankind ought to be cultivated, a thing which Protestants at least do not deny, on what can these faculties be more appropriately exercised by anyone than on the things which concern him so much that it is considered necessary for him to hold opinions on them? If the cultivation of the understanding consists in one thing more than in another, it is surely in learning the grounds of one's own opinions. Whatever people believe, on subjects on which it is of the first importance to believe rightly, they ought to be able to defend against at least the common objections. But, someone may say, "Let them be *taught* the grounds of their opinions. It does not follow that opinions must be merely parroted because they are never heard controverted. Persons who learn geometry do not simply commit the theorems to memory, but understand and learn likewise the demonstrations; and it would be absurd to say that they remain ignorant of the grounds of geometrical truths because they never hear anyone deny and attempt to disprove them." Undoubtedly: and such teaching suffices on a subject like mathematics, where there is nothing at all to be said on the wrong side of the question. The peculiarity of the evidence of mathematical truths is that all the argument is on one side. There are no objections, and no answers to objections. But on every subject on which difference of opinion is possible, the truth depends on a balance to be struck between the two sets of conflicting reasons. Even in natural philosophy, there is always some other explanation possible of the same facts; some geocentric theory instead of heliocentric, some phlogiston instead of oxygen; and it has to be shown why that other theory cannot be the true one; and until this is shown, and until we know how it is shown, we do not understand the grounds of our opinion. But when we turn to subjects infinitely more complicated, to morals, religion, politics, social relations, and the business of life, three-fourths of the arguments for every disputed opinion consist in dispelling the appearances which favor some opinion different from it. The greatest orator, save one, of antiquity, has left it on record that he always studied his adversary's case with as great, if not still greater, intensity than even his own. What Cicero practiced as the means of forensic success requires to be imitated by all who study any subject in order to arrive at the truth. He who knows only his own side of the case knows little of that. His reasons may be good, and no one may have been able to refute them. But if he is equally unable to refute the reasons on the opposite side, if he does not so much as know what they are, he has no ground for preferring either opinion. The rational position for him would be suspension of judgment, and unless he contents himself with that, he is either led by authority or adopts, like the generality of the world, the side to which he feels most inclination. Nor is it enough that he should hear the arguments of adversaries from his own teachers, presented as they state them, and accompanied by what they offer as refutations. That is not the way to do justice to the arguments or bring them into real contact with his own mind. He must be able to hear them from persons who actually believe them, who defend them in earnest and do their very utmost for them. He must know them in their most plausible and persuasive form; he must feel the whole force of the difficulty which the true view of the subject has to encounter and dispose of, else he will never really possess himself of the portion of truth which meets and removes that difficulty. Ninety-nine in a hundred of what are called educated men are in this condition, even of those who can argue fluently for their opinions. Their conclusion may be true, but it might be false for anything they know; they have never thrown themselves into the mental position of those who think differently from them, and considered what such persons may have to say; and, consequently, they do not, in any proper sense of the word, know the doctrine which they themselves profess. They do not know those parts of it which explain and justify the remainder—the considerations which show that a fact which seemingly conflicts with another is reconcilable with it, or that, of two apparently strong reasons, one and not the other ought to be preferred. All that part of the truth which turns the scale and decides the judgment of a completely informed mind, they are strangers to; nor is it ever really known but to those who have attended equally and impartially to both sides and endeavored to see the reasons of both in the strongest light. So essential is this discipline to a real understanding of moral and human subjects that, if opponents of all-important truths do not exist, it is indispensable to imagine them and supply them with the strongest arguments which the most skillful devil's advocate can conjure up.

To abate the force of these considerations, an enemy of free discussion may be supposed to say that there is no necessity for mankind in general to know and understand all that can be said against or for their opinions by philosophers and theologians. That it is not needful for common men to be able to expose all the misstatements or fallacies of an ingenious opponent. That it is enough if there is always somebody capable of answering them, so that nothing likely to mislead uninstructed persons remains unrefuted. That simple minds, having been taught the obvious grounds of the truths inculcated in them, may trust to authority for the rest and, being aware that they have neither knowledge nor talent to resolve every difficulty which can be raised, may repose in the assurance that all those which have been raised have been or can be answered by those who are specially trained to the task.

Conceding to this view of the subject the utmost that can be claimed for it by those most easily satisfied with the amount of understanding of truth which ought to accompany the belief of it, even so, the argument for free discussion is noway weakened. For even this doctrine acknowledges that mankind ought to have a rational assurance that all objections have been satisfactorily answered; and how are they to be answered if that which requires to be answered is not spoken? Or how can the answer be known to be satisfactory if the objectors have no opportunity of showing that it is unsatisfactory? If not the public, at least the philosophers and theologians who are to resolve the difficulties must make themselves familiar with those difficulties in their most puzzling form; and this cannot be accomplished unless they are freely stated and placed in the most advantageous light which they admit of. The Catholic Church has its own way of dealing with this embarrassing problem. It makes a broad separation between those who can be permitted to receive its doctrines on conviction and those who must accept them on trust. Neither, indeed, are allowed any choice as to what they will accept; but the clergy, such at least as can be fully confided in, may admissibly and meritoriously make themselves acquainted with the arguments of opponents, in order to answer them, and may, therefore, read heretical books; the laity, not unless by special permission, hard to be obtained. This discipline recognizes a knowledge of the enemy's case as beneficial to the teachers, but finds means, consistent with this, of denying it to the rest of the world, thus giving to the *élite* more mental culture, though not more mental freedom, than it allows to the mass. By this device it succeeds in obtaining the kind of mental superiority which its purposes require; for though culture without freedom never made a large and liberal mind, it can make a clever *nisi prius* advocate of a cause. But in countries professing Protestantism, this resource is denied, since Protestants hold, at least in theory, that the responsibility for the choice of a religion must be borne by each for himself and cannot be thrown off upon teachers. Besides, in the present state of the world, it is practically impossible that writings which are read by the instructed can be kept from the uninstructed. If the teachers of mankind are to be cognizant of all that they ought to know, everything must be free to be written and published without restraint.

If, however, the mischievous operation of the absence of free discussion, when the received opinions are true, were confined to leaving men ignorant of the grounds of those opinions, it might be thought that this, if an intellectual, is no moral evil and does not affect the worth of the opinions, regarded in their influence on the character. The fact, however, is that not only the grounds of the opinion are forgotten in the absence of discussion, but too often the meaning of the opinion itself. The words which convey it cease to suggest ideas, or suggest only a small portion of those they were originally employed to communicate. Instead of a vivid conception and a living belief, there remain only a few phrases retained by rote; or, if any part, the shell and husk only of the meaning is retained, the finer essence being lost. The great chapter in human history which this fact occupies and fills cannot be too earnestly studied and meditated on.

It is illustrated in the experience of almost all ethical doctrines and religious creeds. They are all full of meaning and vitality to those who originate them, and to the direct disciples of the originators. Their meaning continues to be felt in undiminished strength, and is perhaps brought out into even fuller consciousness, so long as the struggle lasts to give the doctrine or creed an ascendancy over other creeds. At last it either prevails and becomes the general opinion, or its progress stops; it keeps possession of the ground it has gained, but ceases to spread further. When either of these results has become apparent, controversy on the subject flags, and gradually dies away. The doctrine has taken its place, if not as a received opinion, as one of the admitted sects or divisions of opinion; those who hold it have generally inherited, not adopted it; and conversion from one of these doctrines to another, being now an exceptional fact, occupies little place in the thoughts of their professors. Instead of being, as at first, constantly on the alert either to defend themselves against the world or to bring the world over to them, they have subsided into acquiescence and neither listen, when they can help it, to arguments against their creed, nor trouble dissentients (if there be such) with arguments in its favor. From this time may usually be dated the decline in the living power of the doctrine. We often hear the teachers of all creeds lamenting the difficulty of keeping up in the minds of believers a lively apprehension of the truth which they nominally recognize, so that it may penetrate the feelings and acquire a real mastery over the conduct. No such difficulty is complained of while the creed is still fighting for its existence; even the weaker combatants then know and feel what they are fighting for, and the difference between it and other doctrines; and in that period of every creed's existence not a few persons may be found who have realized its fundamental principles in all the forms of thought, have weighed and considered them in all their important bearings, and have experienced the full effect on the character which belief in that creed ought to produce in a mind thoroughly imbued with it. But when it has come to be an hereditary creed, and to be received passively, not actively— when the mind is no longer compelled, in the same degree as at first, to exercise its vital powers on the questions which its belief presents to it, there is a progressive tendency to forget all of the belief except the formularies, or to give it a dull and torpid assent, as if accepting it on trust dispensed with the necessity of realizing it in consciousness, or testing it by personal experience, until it almost ceases to connect itself at all with the inner life of the human being. Then are seen the cases, so frequent in this age of the world as almost to form the majority, in which the creed remains as it were outside the mind, incrusting and petrifying it against all other influences addressed to the higher parts of our nature; manifesting its power by not suffering any fresh and living conviction to get in, but itself doing nothing for the mind or heart except standing sentinel over them to keep them vacant. . . .

. . . All languages and literatures are full of general observations on life, both as to what it is and how to conduct oneself in it—observations which everybody knows, which everybody repeats or hears with acquiescence, which are received as truisms, yet of which most people first truly learn the meaning when experience, generally of a painful kind, has made it a reality to them. How often, when smarting under some unforeseen misfortune or disappointment, does a person call to mind some proverb or common saying, familiar to him all his life, the meaning of which, if he had ever before felt it as he does now, would have saved him from the calamity. There are indeed reasons for this, other than the absence of discussion; there are many truths of which the full meaning *cannot* be realized until personal experience has brought it home. But much more of the meaning even of these would have been understood, and what was understood would have been far more deeply impressed on the mind, if the man had been accustomed to hear it argued *pro* and *con* by people who did understand it. The fatal tendency of mankind to leave off thinking about a thing when it is no longer doubtful is the cause of half their errors. A contemporary author has well spoken of "the deep slumber of a decided opinion."

But what! (it may be asked), Is the absence of unanimity an indispensable condition of true knowledge? Is it necessary that some part of mankind should persist in error to enable any to realize the truth? Does a belief cease to be real and vital as soon as it is generally received—and is a proposition never thoroughly understood and felt unless some doubt of it remains? As soon as mankind have unanimously accepted a truth, does the truth perish within them? The highest aim and best result of improved intelligence, it has hitherto been thought, is to unite mankind more and more in the acknowledgment of all important truths; and does the intelligence only last as long as it has not achieved its object? Do the fruits of conquest perish by the very completeness of the victory?

I affirm no such thing. As mankind improve, the number of doctrines which are no longer disputed or doubted will be constantly on the increase; and the well-being of mankind may almost be measured by the number and gravity of the truths which have reached the point of being uncontested. The cessation, on one question after another, of serious controversy is one of the necessary incidents of the consolidation of opinion—a consolidation as salutary in the case of true opinions as it is dangerous and noxious when the opinions are erroneous. But though this gradual narrowing of the bounds of diversity of opinion is necessary in both senses of the term, being at once inevitable and indispensable, we are not therefore obliged to conclude that all its consequences must be beneficial. The loss of so important an aid to the intelligent and living apprehension of a truth as is afforded by the necessity of explaining it to, or defending it against, opponents, though not sufficient to outweigh, is no trifling drawback from the benefit of its universal recognition. Where this advantage can no longer be had, I confess I should like to see the teachers of mankind endeavoring to provide a substitute for it—some contrivance for making the difficulties of the question as present to the learner's consciousness as if they were pressed upon him by a dissentient champion, eager for his conversion. . . .

. . . If there are any persons who contest a received opinion, or who will do so if law or opinion will let them, let us thank them for it, open our minds to listen to them, and rejoice that there is someone to do for us what we otherwise ought, if we have any regard for either the certainty or the vitality of our convictions, to do with much greater labor for ourselves.

In most controversies there is a mixture of truth and error on the part of each of the contending parties. Communication between them is not for the sake of showing one group to be right and all the others wrong. It is to develop a more comprehensive position, which identifies error, falsehood, and deceit wherever they occur and which draws upon strength of argument whenever it can be found. Communication between different groups also tends to ensure that legitimate interests continue to be heard. Mill is not hoping for an eventual condition in which there will be no further clash of argument.

Notice that Mill thinks of the discovery of truth in public discourse exclusively as a function of the juxtaposition of antecedent, but partial, truths. He does not formulate the notion of a hypothesis that would prescribe a novel reconstruction of events. Such hypotheses, Dewey would later urge, are the principal means for discovering nature's potentialities; and they are likewise the principal means for addressing new problems and for contriving new solutions to old problems.

It still remains to speak of one of the principal causes which make diversity of opinion advantageous, and will continue to do so until mankind shall have entered a stage of intellectual advancement which at present seems at an incalculable distance. We have hitherto considered only two possibilities: that the received opinion may be false, and some other opinion, consequently, true; or that, the received opinion being true, a conflict with the opposite error is essential to a clear apprehension and deep feeling of its truth. But there is a commoner case than either of these: when the conflicting doctrines, instead of being one true and the other false, share the truth between them, and the nonconforming opinion is needed to supply the remainder of the truth of which the received doctrine embodies only a part. Popular opinions, on subjects not palpable to sense, are often true, but seldom or never the whole truth. They are a part of the truth, sometimes a greater, sometimes a smaller part, but exaggerated, distorted, and disjointed from the truths by which they ought to be accompanied and limited. Heretical opinions, on the other hand, are generally some of these suppressed and neglected truths, bursting the bonds which kept them down, and either seeking reconciliation with the truth contained in the common opinion, or fronting it as enemies, and setting themselves up, with similar exclusiveness, as the whole truth. The latter case is hitherto the most frequent, as, in the human mind, one-sidedness has always been the rule, and many-sidedness the exception. Hence, even in revolutions of opinion, one part of the truth usually sets while another rises. Even progress, which ought to superadd, for the most part only substitutes one partial and incomplete truth for another; improvement consisting chiefly in this, that the new fragment of truth is more wanted, more adapted to the needs of the time than that which it displaces. Such being the partial character of prevailing opinions, even when resting on a true foundation, every opinion which embodies somewhat of the portion of truth which the common opinion omits ought to be considered precious, with whatever amount of error and confusion that truth may be blended. No sober judge of human affairs will feel bound to be indignant because those who force on our notice truths which we should otherwise have overlooked, overlook some of those which we see. Rather, he will think that so long as popular truth is one-sided, it is more desirable than otherwise that unpopular truth should have one-sided assertors, too, such being usually the most energetic and the most likely to compel reluctant attention to the fragment of wisdom which they proclaim as if it were the whole.

Thus, in the eighteenth century, when nearly all the instructed, and all those of the uninstructed who were led by them, were lost in admiration of what is called civilization, and of the marvels of modern science, literature, and philosophy, and while greatly overrating the amount of unlikeness between the men of modern and those of ancient times, indulged the belief that the whole of the difference was in their own favor; with what a salutary shock did the paradoxes of Rousseau explode like bombshells in the midst, dislocating the compact mass of one-sided opinion and forcing its elements to recombine in a better form and with additional ingredients. Not that the current opinions were on the whole farther from the truth than Rousseau's were; on the contrary, they were nearer to it; they contained more of positive truth, and very much less of error. Nevertheless there lay in Rousseau's doctrine, and has floated down the stream of opinion along with it, a considerable amount of exactly those truths which the popular opinion wanted; and these are the deposit which was left behind them when the flood subsided. The superior worth of simplicity of life, the enervating and demoralizing effect of the trammels and hypocrisies of artificial society are ideas which have never been entirely absent from cultivated minds since Rousseau wrote; and they will in time produce their due effect, though at present needing to be asserted as much as ever, and to be asserted by deeds; for words, on this subject, have nearly exhausted their power.

In politics, again, it is almost a commonplace that a party of order or stability and a party of progress or reform are both necessary elements of a healthy state of political life, until the one or the other shall have so enlarged its mental grasp as to be a party equally of order and of progress, knowing and distinguishing what is fit to be preserved from what ought to be swept away. Each of these modes of thinking derives its utility from the deficiencies of the other; but it is in a great measure the opposition of the other that keeps each within the limits of reason and sanity. Unless opinions favorable to democracy and to aristocracy, to property and to equality, to co-operation and to competition, to luxury and to abstinence, to sociality and individuality, to liberty and discipline, and all the other standing antagonisms of practical life, are expressed with equal freedom and enforced and defended with equal talent and energy, there is no chance of both elements obtaining their due; one scale is sure to go up, and the other down. Truth, in the great practical concerns of life, is so much a question of the reconciling and combining of opposites that very few have minds sufficiently capacious and impartial to make the adjustment with an approach to correctness, and it has to be made by the rough process of a struggle between combatants fighting under hostile banners. On any of the great open questions just enumerated, if either of the two opinions has a better claim than the other, not merely to be tolerated, but to be encouraged and countenanced, it is the one which happens at the particular time and place to be in a minority. That is the opinion which, for the time being, represents the neglected interests, the side of human well-being which is in danger of obtaining less than its share. I am aware that there is not, in this country, any intolerance of differences of opinion on most of these topics. They are adduced to show, by admitted and multiplied examples, the universality of the fact that only through diversity of opinion is there, in the existing state of human intellect, a chance of fair play to all sides of the truth. When there are persons to be found who form an exception to the apparent unanimity of the world on any subject, even if the world is in the right, it is always probable that dissentients have something worth hearing to say for themselves, and that truth would lose something by their silence. . . .

I do not pretend that the most unlimited use of the freedom of enunciating all possible opinions would put an end to the evils of religious or philosophical sectarianism. Every truth which men of narrow capacity are in earnest about is sure to be asserted, inculcated, and in many ways even acted on, as if no other truth existed in the world, or at all events none that could limit or qualify the first. I acknowledge that the tendency of all opinions to become sectarian is not cured by the freest discussion, but is often heightened and exacerbated thereby; the truth which ought to have been, but was not, seen, being rejected all the more violently because proclaimed by persons regarded as opponents. But it is not on the impassioned partisan, it is on the calmer and more disinterested bystander, that this collision of opinions works its salutary effect. Not the violent conflict between parts of the truth, but the quiet suppression of half of it, is the formidable evil; there is always hope when people are forced to listen to both sides; it is when they attend only to one that errors harden into prejudices, and truth itself ceases to have the effect of truth by being exaggerated into falsehood. And since there are few mental attributes more rare than that judicial faculty which can sit in intelligent judgment between two sides of a question, of which only one is represented by an advocate before it, truth has no chance but in proportion as every side of it, every opinion which embodies any fraction of the truth, not only finds advocates, but is so advocated as to be listened to.

Mill summarizes his arguments. His first statement makes it clear that his paramount concern is with the full development of all individuals. He believes that freedom of thought and expression is the prime condition of the flourishing of human individuality and human progress.

He adds to his summary a few remarks about the kind of personal behavior that is necessary to make this freedom effective. His demands seem so reasonable! If we take notice, however, of the tactics of many of our educators, editorial writers, news reporters, and intellectuals (to say nothing of all those who are overtly engaged in politics), we shall see few traces of Mill's influence.

We have now recognized the necessity to the mental well-being of mankind (on which all their other well-being depends) of freedom of opinion, and freedom of the expression of opinion, on four distinct grounds, which we will now briefly recapitulate:

First, if any opinion is compelled to silence, that opinion may, for aught we can certainly know, be true. To deny this is to assume our own infallibility.

Secondly, though the silenced opinion be an error, it may, and very commonly does, contain a portion of truth; and since the general or prevailing opinion on any subject is rarely or never the whole truth, it is only by the collision of adverse opinions that the remainder of the truth has any chance of being supplied.

Thirdly, even if the received opinion be not only true, but the whole truth; unless it is suffered to be, and actually is, vigorously and earnestly contested, it will, by most of those who receive it, be held in the manner of a prejudice, with little comprehension or feeling of its rational grounds. And not only this, but, fourthly, the meaning of the doctrine itself will be in danger of being lost or enfeebled, and deprived of its vital effect on the character and conduct: the dogma becoming a mere formal profession, inefficacious for good, but cumbering the ground and preventing the growth of any real and heartfelt conviction from reason or personal experience.

Before quitting the subject of freedom of opinion, it is fit to take some notice of those who say that the free expression of all opinions should be permitted on condition that the manner be temperate, and do not pass the bounds of fair discussion. Much might be said on the impossibility of fixing where these supposed bounds are to be placed; for if the test be offense to those whose opinions are attacked, I think experience testifies that this offense is given whenever the attack is telling and powerful, and that every opponent who pushes them hard, and whom they find it difficult to answer, appears to them, if he shows any strong feeling on the subject, an intemperate opponent. But this, though an important consideration in a practical point of view, merges in a more fundamental objection. Undoubtedly, the manner of asserting an opinion, even though it be a true one, may be very objectionable and may justly incur severe censure. But the principal offenses of the kind are such as it is mostly impossible, unless by accidental self-betrayal, to bring home to conviction. The gravest of them is, to argue sophistically, to suppress facts or arguments, to misstate the elements of the case, or misrepresent the opposite opinion. But all this, even to the most aggravated degree, is so continually done in perfect good faith by persons who are not considered, and in many other respects may not deserve to be considered, ignorant or incompetent, that it is rarely possible, on adequate grounds, conscientiously to stamp the misrepresentation as morally culpable, and still less could law presume to interfere with this kind of controversial misconduct. With regard to what is commonly meant by intemperate discussion, namely invective, sarcasm, personality, and the like, the denunciation of these weapons would deserve more sympathy if it were ever proposed to interdict them equally to both sides; but it is only desired to restrain the employment of them against the prevailing opinion; against the unprevailing they may not only be used without general disapproval, but will be likely to obtain for him who uses them the praise of honest zeal and righteous indignation. Yet whatever mischief arises from their use is greatest when they are employed against the comparatively defenseless; and whatever unfair advantage can be derived by any opinion from this mode of asserting it accrues almost exclusively to received opinions. The worst offense of this kind which can be committed by a polemic is to stigmatize those who hold the contrary opinion as bad and immoral men. To calumny of this sort, those who hold any unpopular opinion are peculiarly exposed, because they are in general few and uninfluential, and nobody but themselves feels much interested in seeing justice done them; but this weapon is, from the nature of the case, denied to those who attack a prevailing opinion; they can neither use it with safety to themselves, nor, if they could, would it do anything but recoil on their own cause. In general, opinions contrary to those commonly received can only obtain a hearing by studied moderation of language and the most cautious avoidance of unnecessary offense, from which they hardly ever deviate even in a slight degree without losing ground, while unmeasured vituperation employed on the side of the prevailing opinion really does deter people from professing contrary opinions and from listening to those who profess them. For the interest, therefore, of truth and justice it is far more important to restrain this employment of vituperative language than the other; and, for example, if it were necessary to choose, there would be much more need to discourage offensive attacks on infidelity than on religion. It is, however, obvious that law and authority have no business with restraining either, while opinion ought, in every instance, to determine its verdict by the circumstances of the individual case—condemning everyone, on whichever side of the argument he places himself, in whose mode of advocacy either want of candor, or malignity, bigotry, or intolerance of feeling manifest themselves; but not inferring these vices from the side which a person takes, though it be the contrary side of the question to our own; and giving merited honor to everyone, whatever opinion he may hold, who has calmness to see and honesty to state what his opponents and their opinions really are, exaggerating nothing to their discredit, keeping nothing back which tells, or can be supposed to tell, in their favor. This is the real morality of public discussion; and if often violated, I am happy to think that there are many controversialists who to a great extent observe it, and a still greater number who conscientiously strive toward it.

John Dewey

Excerpts on Social Intelligence

Dewey revered the work of his predecessors in their struggles for liberty. "I would not in the least disparage," he wrote, "the noble fight waged by early liberals in behalf of individual freedom of thought and expression. We owe more to them than it is possible to record in words" (Dewey, 1935/1963b, p. 66). He thought of himself as building upon their work (as well as upon other traditions in philosophy). He believed they had deficient notions of the individual and society, and consequently a deficient notion of freedom; and he tried to correct and enrich these ideas. In the present text we are concerned with excellence in public discourse. Dewey's work on this theme relative to Mill and other liberals was of the same nature. Mill's defense of freedom of speech, for example, was sound as far as it went, but it did not go far enough. Excellence in democratic discourse cannot be attained until there are social agencies (public or private) actively devoted to the formation of the human resources needed to make effective use of the sort of freedom that Mill had defended. In addition, we must attain a conception of discourse that goes beyond that which Mill had assumed. Due to his philosophic presuppositions, Mill had thought of discourse exclusively as a method of criticism. Taking experimental science as his model, Dewey pointed out that effective inquiry requires creativity in the formulation of plans of action. These plans call for deliberate reconstruction of existing circumstances in order to manage ongoing affairs in service of human needs and aspirations.

The selections have been edited to present Dewey's analyses of the nature and conditions of excellence in public discourse. He believed that the method of social intelligence does not presuppose definite answers to questions of public policy. From instance to instance, it might yield now a "liberal" another time a "conservative" solution, and then again a "radical" or a "reactionary" outcome. The important matter is the use of the method, and not adherence to antecedent doctrines, however they might be labeled. Accordingly, the explication of social intelligence should not be diverted or prejudiced by the needless introduction of heated issues. But Dewey's writings are seldom concentrated on questions of method alone. They are bulging with critiques of political, social, and economic conditions; and there is ever-present polemic with all points on the political compass. This mixture of issues poses editorial problems. So far as possible, I have eliminated irrelevant polemic, and I have reduced social analyses that do not bear directly on the issues of the nature and conditions of social intelligence.[1] The titles provided for each section of this appendix are my own.

1. THE SCIENTIFIC APPROACH
TO PROBLEM SOLVING

In this brief excerpt from Individualism, Old and New *(1930a, pp. 119–20), Dewey asserts that a scientific approach to social problems excludes wholesale system building or adherence to antecedently given systems of thought.*

Because science starts with questions and inquiries it is fatal to all social system-making and programs of fixed ends. In spite of the bankruptcy of past systems of belief, it is hard to surrender our faith in system and in some wholesale belief. We continually reason as if the difficulty were in the particular system that has failed and as if we were on the point of now finally hitting upon one that is true as all the others were false. The real trouble is with the attitude of dependence upon any of them. Scientific method would teach us to break up, to inquire definitely and with particularity, to seek solutions in the terms of concrete problems as they arise. It is not easy to imagine the difference which would follow from the shift of thought to discrimination and analysis. Wholesale creeds and all-inclusive ideals are impotent in the face of actual situations; for doing always means the doing of something in particular. They are worse than impotent. They conduce to blind and vague emotional states in which credulity is at home, and where action, following the lead of overpowering emotion, is easily manipulated by the self-seekers who have kept their heads and wits. Nothing would conduce more, for example, to the elimination of war than the substitution of specific analysis of its causes for the wholesale love of "liberty, humanity, justice and civilization."

All of these considerations would lead to the conclusion that depression of the individual is the individual's own liability, were it not for the time it takes for a new principle to make its way deeply into individual mind on a large scale. But as time goes on, the responsibility becomes an individual one. For individuality is inexpugnable and it is of its nature to assert itself. The first move in recovery of an integrated individual is accordingly with the individual himself. In whatever occupation he finds himself and whatever interest concerns him, he is himself and no other, and he lives in situations that are in some respect flexible and plastic.

We are given to thinking of society in large and vague ways. We should forget "society" and think of law, industry, religion, medicine, politics, art, education, philosophy—and think of them in the plural. For points of contact are not the same for any two persons, and hence the questions which the interests and occupations pose are never twice the same. There is no contact so immutable that it will not yield at some point. All these callings and concerns are the avenues through which the world acts upon us and we upon the world. There is no society at large, no business in general. Harmony with conditions is not a single and monotonous uniformity, but a diversified affair requiring individual attack.

2. KNOWLEDGE AND ACTION

The following excerpts from The Quest for Certainty *provide a summary account of experimental method and its relation to action. Dewey refers to the relation between knowledge and the values that guide conduct. He had the deepest opposition to the view that we might derive value judgments from scientific propositions. Rather, we use scientific method to determine how the pursuit of particular values might serve to reconstruct a given problematic situation in a manner that would be satisfying and fulfilling to its participants. An experimental hypothesis would prescribe the changes that need to be introduced in order to transform the situation from problematic to consummatory. Just as in science, creativity in the formation of hypotheses is one of our most valuable resources.*[2]

. . . What is the bearing of our existential knowledge at any time, the most dependable knowledge afforded by inquiry, upon our judgments and beliefs about the ends and means which are to direct our conduct? What does knowledge indicate about the authoritative guidance of our desires and affections, our plans and policies? Unless knowledge gives some regulation, the only alternative is to fall back on custom, external pressure and free play of impulse. . . .

But the situation has a still more unfortunate phase. For it signifies intellectual confusion, practically chaos, in respect to the criteria and principles which are employed in framing judgments and reaching conclusions upon things of most vital importance. It signifies the absence of intellectual authority. Old beliefs have dissolved as far as definite operative hold upon the regulation of criticism and the formation of plans and policies, working ideals and ends, is concerned. And there is nothing else to take their place.

When I say "authority" I do not mean a fixed set of doctrines by which to settle mechanically problems as they arise. Such authority is dogmatic, not intellectual. I mean *methods* congruous with those used in scientific inquiry and adopting their conclusions; methods to be used in directing criticism and in forming the ends and purposes that are acted upon. We have obtained in constantly accelerated measure in the last few centuries a large amount of sound beliefs regarding the world in which we live; we have ascertained much that is new and striking about life and man. On the other hand, men have desires and affections, hopes and fears, purposes and intentions which influence the most important actions performed. These need intellectual direction. Why has modern philosophy contributed so little to bring about an integration between what we know about the world and the intelligent direction of what we do? The purport of this chapter is to show that the cause resides in unwillingness to surrender two ideas formulated in conditions which both intellectually and practically were very different from those in which we now live. These two ideas, to repeat, are that knowledge is concerned with disclosure of the characteristics of antecedent existences and essences, and that the properties of value found therein provide the authoritative standards for the conduct of life.

Both of these traits are due to quest for certainty by cognitive means which exclude practical activity—namely, one which effects actual and concrete modifications in existence. Practical activity suffers from a double discrediting because of the perpetuation of these two features of tradition. It is a mere external follower upon knowledge, having no part in its determination. Instead of evolving its own standards and ends in its own developing processes, it is supposed to conform to what is fixed in the antecedent structure of things. Herein we locate the source of that internal division which was said to characterize modern philosophic thought. It accepts the conclusions of scientific inquiry without remaking the conceptions of mind, knowledge and the character of the object of knowledge that are involved in the methods by which these conclusions are reached.

The chapters of which this is the concluding portion are introductory. They have tried to make clear a problem and the reasons why it is a problem. If, as has been intimated, the problem arises from continued adherence to certain conceptions framed centuries ago and then embodied in the entire western tradition, the problem is artificial in as far as it would not arise from reflection upon actual conditions of science and life. The next task is accordingly to elucidate the reconstructions of tradition which are involved in the actual procedure and results of knowing, as this is exemplified in physical inquiry. The latter is taken as the type and pattern of knowing since it is the most perfected of all branches of intellectual inquiry. . . . Having discovered what knowledge means in its own terms, that is, in those of the conduct of knowing as a going concern, we shall be ready to appreciate the great transformation that is demanded in the older notions of mind and knowledge. Particularly we shall see how completely the separation of knowing and doing from one another has broken down. The conclusion of this part of the discussion will be that standards and tests of validity are found in the consequences of overt activity, not in what is fixed prior to it and independently of it. . . .

In the old scheme, knowledge, as science, signified precisely and exclusively turning away from change to the changeless. In the new experimental science, knowledge is obtained in exactly the opposite way, namely, through deliberate institution of a definite and specified course of change. *The* method of physical inquiry is to introduce some change in order to see what other change ensues; the correlation between these changes, when measured by a series of operations, constitutes the definite and desired object of knowledge. . . .

While the traits of experimental inquiry are familiar, so little use has been made of them in formulating a theory of knowledge and of mind in relation to nature that a somewhat explicit statement of well known facts is excusable. They exhibit three outstanding characteristics. The first is the obvious one that all experimentation involves *overt* doing, the making of definite changes in the environment or in our relation to it. The second is that experiment is not a random activity but is directed by ideas which have to meet the conditions set by the need of the problem inducing the active inquiry. The third and concluding feature, in which the other two receive their full measure of meaning, is that the outcome of the directed activity is the construction of a new empirical situation in which objects are differently related to one another, and such that the *consequences* of directed operations form the objects that have the property of being *known*.

The rudimentary prototype of experimental doing for the sake of knowing is found in ordinary procedures. When we are trying to make out the nature of a confused and unfamiliar object, we perform various acts with a view to establishing a new relationship to it, such as will bring to light qualities which will aid in understanding it. We turn it over, bring it into a better light, rattle and shake it, thump, push and press it, and so on. The object as it is experienced prior to the introduction of these changes baffles us; the intent of these acts is to make changes which will elicit some previously unperceived qualities, and by varying conditions of perception shake loose some property which as it stands blinds or misleads us. . . .

The remarkable difference between the attitude which accepts the objects of ordinary perception, use and enjoyment as final, as culminations of natural processes and that which takes them as starting points for reflection and investigation, is one which reaches far beyond the technicalities of science. It marks a revolution in the whole spirit of life, in the entire attitude taken toward whatever is found in existence. When the things which exist around us, which we touch, see, hear and taste are regarded as interrogations for which an answer must be sought (and must be sought by means of deliberate introduction of changes till they are reshaped into something different), nature as it already exists ceases to be something which must be accepted and submitted to, endured or enjoyed, just as it is. It is now something to be modified, to be intentionally controlled. It is material to act upon so as to transform it into new objects which better answer our needs. Nature as it exists at any particular time is a challenge, rather than a completion; it provides possible starting points and opportunities rather than final ends.

In short, there is a change from knowing as an esthetic enjoyment of the properties of nature regarded as a work of divine art, to knowing as a means of secular control—that is, a method of purposefully introducing changes which will alter the direction of the course of events. Nature as it exists at a given time is material for arts to be brought to bear upon it to reshape it, rather than already a finished work of art. Thus the changed attitude toward change to which reference was made has a much wider meaning than that which the new science offered as a technical pursuit. When correlations of changes are made the goal of knowledge, the fulfillment of its aim in discovery of these correlations is equivalent to placing in our hands an instrument of control. When one change is given, and we know with measured accuracy its connection with another change, we have the potential means of producing or averting that other event. The esthetic attitude is of necessity directed to what is already there; to what is finished, complete. The attitude of control looks to the future; to production.

The same point is stated in another way in saying that the reduction of given objects to data for a knowing or an investigation still to be undertaken liberates man from subjection to the past. The scientific attitude, as an attitude of interest in change instead of interest in isolated and complete fixities, is necessarily alert for problems; every new question is an opportunity for further experimental inquiries— for effecting more directed change. . . .

Sensory qualities experienced through vision have their cognitive status and office, not (as sensational empiricism holds) in and of themselves in isolation, or as merely forced upon attention, but because they are the consequences of definite and intentionally performed operations. Only in connection with the intent, or idea, of these operations do they amount to anything, either as disclosing any fact or giving test and proof of any theory. The rationalist school was right in as far as it insisted that sensory qualities are significant for knowledge only when connected by means of ideas. But they were wrong in locating the connecting ideas in intellect apart from experience. Connection is instituted through operations which define ideas, and operations are as much matters of experience as are sensory qualities.

It is not too much to say, therefore, that for the first time there is made possible an empirical theory of ideas free from the burdens imposed alike by sensationalism and *a priori* rationalism. This accomplishment is, I make bold to say, one of three or four outstanding feats of intellectual history. For it emancipates us from the supposed need of always harking back to what has already been given, something had by alleged direct or immediate knowledge in the past, for the test of the value of ideas. A definition of the nature of ideas in terms of operations to be performed and the test of the validity of the ideas by the *consequences* of these operations establishes connectivity within concrete experience. At the same time, by emancipation of thinking from the necessity of testing its conclusions solely by reference to antecedent existence it makes clear the originative possibilities of thinking. . . .

This phase of the discussion is not complete till it has been explicitly noted that all general conceptions (ideas, theories, thought) are hypothetical. Ability to frame hypotheses is the means by which man is liberated from submergence in the existences that surround him and that play upon him physically and sensibly. It is the positive phase of abstraction. But hypotheses are conditional; they have to be tested by the consequences of the operations they define and direct. The discovery of the value of hypothetical ideas when employed to suggest and direct concrete processes, and the vast extension of this operation in the modern history of science, mark a great emancipation and correspondent increase of intellectual control. But their final value is not determined by their internal elaboration and consistency, but by the consequences they effect in existence as that is perceptibly experienced. Scientific conceptions are not a revelation of prior and independent reality. They are a system of hypotheses, worked out under conditions of definite test, by means of which our intellectual and practical traffic with nature is rendered freer, more secure and more significant.

3. DEMOCRACY AND THE SCIENTIFIC ATTITUDE

The next passages are taken from Freedom and Culture *(1939/1963a, pp. 145–51). The focus of attention is not scientific method, but the scientific attitude, which is indispensable if democracy is ever to rise above partisan squabbles.*

We have been considering science as a body of conclusions. We have ignored science in its quality of an attitude embodied in habitual will to employ certain methods of observation, reflection, and test rather than others. When we look at science from this point of view, the significance of science as a constituent of culture takes on a new color. The great body of scientific inquirers would deny with indignation that they are actuated in *their* esteem for science by its material serviceability. If they use words sanctioned by long tradition, they say they are moved by love of the truth. If they use contemporary phraseology, less grandiloquent in sound but of equivalent meaning, they say they are moved by a controlling interest in inquiry, in discovery, in following where the evidence of discovered facts points.

Above all they say that this kind of interest excludes interest in reaching any conclusion not warranted by evidence, no matter how personally congenial it may be.

In short, it is a fact that a certain group of men, perhaps relatively not very numerous, have a "disinterested" interest in scientific inquiry. This interest has developed a morale having its own distinctive features. Some of its obvious elements are willingness to hold belief in suspense, ability to doubt until evidence is obtained; willingness to go where evidence points instead of putting first a personally preferred conclusion; ability to hold ideas in solution and use them as hypotheses to be tested instead of as dogmas to be asserted; and (possibly the most distinctive of all) enjoyment of new fields for inquiry and of new problems.

Every one of these traits goes contrary to some human impulse that is naturally strong. Uncertainty is disagreeable to most persons; suspense is so hard to endure that assured expectation of an unfortunate outcome is usually preferred to a long-continued state of doubt. "Wishful thinking" is a comparatively modern phrase; but men upon the whole have usually believed what they wanted to believe, except as very convincing evidence made it impossible. Apart from a scientific attitude, guesses, with persons left to themselves, tend to become opinions and opinions dogmas. To hold theories and principles in solution, awaiting confirmation, goes contrary to the grain. Even today questioning a statement made by a person is often taken by him as a reflection upon his integrity, and is resented. For many millennia opposition to views widely held in a community was intolerable. It called down the wrath of the deities who are in charge of the group. Fear of the unknown, fear of change and novelty, tended, at all times before the rise of scientific attitude, to drive men into rigidity of beliefs and habits; they entered upon unaccustomed lines of behavior—even in matters of minor moment—with qualms which exacted rites of expiation. Exceptions to accepted rules have either been ignored or systematically explained away when they were too conspicuous to ignore. Baconian idols of the tribe, the cave, the theater, and den have caused men to rush to conclusions, and then to use all their powers to defend from criticism and change the conclusions arrived at. The connection of common law with custom and its resistance to change are familiar facts. Even religious beliefs and rites which were at first more or less heretical deviations harden into modes of action it is impious to question, after once they have become part of the habits of a group.

If I mention such familiar considerations it is in part to suggest that we may well be grateful that science has had undeniable social serviceability, and that to some extent and in some places strong obstructions to adoption of changed beliefs have been overcome. But the chief reason for calling attention to them is the proof they furnish that in some persons and to some degree science has already created a new morale—which is equivalent to the creation of new desires and new ends. The existence of the scientific attitude and spirit, even upon a limited scale, is proof that science is capable of developing a distinctive type of disposition and purpose: a type that goes far beyond provision of more effective means for realizing desires which exist independently of any effect of science.

It is not becoming, to put it moderately, for those who are themselves animated by the scientific morale to assert that other persons are incapable of coming into possession of it and being moved by it.

Such an attitude is saved from being professional snobbery only when it is the result of sheer thoughtlessness. When one and the same representative of the intellectual class denounces any view that attaches inherent importance to the consequences of science, claiming the view is false to the spirit of science—and also holds that it is impossible for science to do anything to affect desires and ends, the inconsistency demands explanation.

A situation in which the fundamental dispositions and ends of a few are influenced by science while that of most persons and most groups is not so influenced proves that the issue is cultural. The difference sets a social problem: what are the causes for the existence of this great gap, especially since it has such serious consequences? If it is possible for persons to have their beliefs formed on the ground of evidence, procured by systematic and competent inquiry, nothing can be more disastrous socially than that the great majority of persons should have them formed by habit, accidents of circumstance, propaganda, personal and class bias. The existence, even on a relatively narrow scale, of a morale of fairmindedness, intellectual integrity, of will to subordinate personal preference to ascertained facts and to share with others what is found out, instead of using it for personal gain, is a challenge of the most searching kind. Why don't a great many more persons have this attitude?

The answer given to this challenge is bound up with the fate of democracy. The spread of literacy, the immense extension of the influence of the press in books, newspapers, periodicals, make the issue peculiarly urgent for a democracy. The very agencies that a century and a half ago were looked upon as those that were sure to advance the cause of democratic freedom, are those which now make it possible to create pseudo-public opinion and to undermine democracy from within. Callousness due to continuous reiteration may produce a certain immunity to the grosser kinds of propaganda. But in the long run negative measures afford no assurance. While it would be absurd to believe it desirable or possible for every one to become a scientist when science is defined from the side of subject matter, the future of democracy is allied with spread of the scientific attitude. It is the sole guarantee against wholesale misleading by propaganda. More important still, it is the only assurance of the possibility of a public opinion intelligent enough to meet present social problems.

To become aware of the problem is a condition of taking steps toward its solution. The problem is in part economic. The nature of control of the means of publicity enters directly; sheer financial control is not a favorable sign. The democratic belief in free speech, free press and free assembly is one of the things that exposes democratic institutions to attack. For representatives of totalitarian states, who are the first to deny such freedom when they are in power, shrewdly employ it in a democratic country to destroy the foundations of democracy. Backed with the necessary financial means, they are capable of carrying on a work of continuous sapping and mining. More dangerous, perhaps, in the end is the fact that all economic conditions tending toward centralization and concentration of the means of production and distribution affect the public press, whether individuals so desire or not. The causes which require large corporate capital to carry on modern business, naturally influence the publishing business.

The problem is also an educative one. A book instead of a paragraph could be given to this aspect of the topic. That the schools have mostly been given to imparting information ready-made, along with teaching the tools of literacy, cannot be denied. The methods used in acquiring such information are not those which develop skill in inquiry and in test of opinions. On the contrary, they are positively hostile to it. They tend to dull native curiosity, and to load powers of observation and experimentation with such a mass of unrelated material that they do not operate as effectively as they do in many an illiterate person. The problem of the common schools in a democracy has reached only its first stage when they are provided for everybody. Until what shall be taught and how it is taught is settled upon the basis of formation of the scientific attitude, the so-called educational work of schools is a dangerously hit-or-miss affair as far as democracy is concerned.

The problem—as was suggested earlier—is also one of art. It is difficult to write briefly on this aspect of the question without giving rise to false impressions. For of late there has been an active campaign, carried on in the name of the social function of art, for using the arts, the plastic arts as well as literature, in propaganda for special views which are dogmatically asserted to be socially necessary. In consequence, any reference to the topic may seem to have a flavor of commendation of something of the same kind, only exercised by way of a counter-campaign in behalf of democratic ideas. The point is different. It is a reminder that ideas are effective not as bare ideas but as they have imaginative content and emotional appeal. I have alluded to the extensive reaction that has set in against the earlier over-simplified rationalism. The reaction tended to go to an opposite extreme. In emphasizing the role of wants, impulse, habit, and emotion, it often denied any efficacy whatever to ideas, to intelligence. The problem is that of effecting the union of ideas and knowledge with the non-rational factors in the human make-up. Art is the name given to all the agencies by which this union is effected.

The problem is also a moral and religious one. That religions have operated most effectively in alliance with the fine arts was indicated earlier. Yet the historic influence of religions has often been to magnify doctrines that are not subject to critical inquiry and test. Their cumulative effect in producing habits of mind at odds with the attitudes required for maintenance of democracy is probably much greater than is usually recognized. Shrewd observers have said that one factor in the relatively easy victory of totalitarianism in Germany was the void left by decay of former theological beliefs. Those who had lost one external authority upon which they had depended were ready to turn to another one which was closer and more tangible.

To say that the issue is a moral one is to say that in the end it comes back to personal choice and action. From one point of view everything which has been said is a laboring of the commonplace that democratic government is a function of public opinion and public sentiment. But identification of its formation in the democratic direction with democratic extension of the scientific morale till it is part of the ordinary equipment of the ordinary individual indicates the issue is a moral one. It is individual persons who need to have this attitude substituted for pride and prejudice, for class and personal interest, for beliefs made dear by custom and early emotional associations. It is only by the choice and the active endeavor of many individuals that this result can be effected.

4. IDEAS AND SOCIAL CHANGE

The following selections say much about liberalism, both in the way of criticism of the liberal tradition and in the formulation of an enlarged liberalism. The core of liberalism as Dewey conceives it is adoption of the method of intelligence for the purpose of expanding and enriching freedom and individuality. These aims should not be thought of as the exclusive possession of liberalism. One need not be a liberal in the conventional political sense to endorse either the method or the aims.

Acutely conscious of historical change, Dewey proposes that the method mediate between the values and achievements of our inheritance and the new demands and opportunities that change inevitably brings. Experimental plans of action must be formulated in cognizance of the actual resources and limitations of a problematic situation, and they must be determined by a consultative process, rather than being imposed by an elite. Here Dewey parts company with conservatives and Marxists, if the former are adamant that we use old approaches to new problems, no matter what, and if the latter are insistent that social change conform to an antecedently fixed and given blueprint. All selections in this section are from Liberalism and Social Action.[3]

The net effect of the struggle of early liberals to emancipate individuals from restrictions imposed upon them by the inherited type of social organization was to pose a problem, that of a new social organization. The ideas of liberals set forth in the first third of the nineteenth century were potent in criticism and in analysis. They released forces that had been held in check. But analysis is not construction, and release of force does not of itself give direction to the force that is set free. Victorian optimism concealed for a time the crisis at which liberalism had arrived. But when that optimism vanished amid the conflict of nations, classes and races characteristic of the latter part of the nineteenth century—a conflict that has grown more intense with the passing years—the crisis could no longer be covered up. The beliefs and methods of earlier liberalism were ineffective when faced with the problems of social organization and integration. Their inadequacy is a large part of belief now so current that all liberalism is an outmoded doctrine. At the same time, insecurity and uncertainty in belief and purpose are powerful factors in generating dogmatic faiths that are profoundly hostile to everything to which liberalism in any possible formulation is devoted. . . .

. . . The problem of achieving freedom was immeasurably widened and deepened. It did not now present itself as a conflict between government and the liberty of individuals in matters of conscience and economic action, but as a problem of establishing an entire social order, possessed of a spiritual authority that would nurture and direct the inner as well as the outer life of individuals. The problem of science was no longer merely technological applications for increase of material productivity, but imbuing the minds of individuals with the spirit of reasonableness, fostered by social organization and contributing to its development. The problem of democracy was seen to be not solved, hardly more than externally touched, by the establishment of universal suffrage and representative government. As Havelock Ellis has said, "We see now that the vote and the ballot-box do not make the voter free from even external pressure; and, which is of much more consequence, they do not necessarily free him from his own slavish instincts." The problem of democracy becomes the problem of that form of social organization, extending to all the areas and ways of living, in which the powers of individuals shall not be merely released from mechanical external constraint but shall be fed, sustained and directed. Such an organization demands much more of education than general schooling, which without a renewal of the springs of purpose and desire becomes a new mode of mechanization and formalization, as hostile to liberty as ever was governmental constraint. It demands of science much more than external technical application—which again leads to mechanization of life and results in a new kind of enslavement. It demands that the method of inquiry, of discrimination, of test by verifiable consequences, be naturalized in all the matters, of large and of detailed scope, that arise for judgment. . . . If we strip its creed from adventitious elements, there are . . . enduring values for which earlier liberalism stood. These values are liberty; the development of the inherent capacities of individuals made possible through liberty, and the central rôle of free intelligence in inquiry, discussion and expression. . . .

Before considering the three values, it is advisable to note one adventitious idea that played a large rôle in the later incapacitation of liberalism. The earlier liberals lacked historic sense and interest. For a while this lack had an immediate pragmatic value. It gave liberals a powerful weapon in their fight with reactionaries. For it enabled them to undercut the appeal to origin, precedent and past history by which the opponents of social change gave sacrosanct quality to existing inequities and abuses. But disregard of history took its revenge. It blinded the eyes of liberals to the fact that their own special interpretations of liberty, individuality and intelligence were themselves historically conditioned, and were relevant only to their own time. They put forward their ideas as immutable truths good at all times and places; they had no idea of historic relativity, either in general or in its application to themselves. . . .

. . . Grateful recognition is due early liberals for their valiant battle in behalf of freedom of thought, conscience, expression and communication. The civil liberties we possess, however precariously today, are in large measure the fruit of their efforts and those of the French liberals who engaged in the same battle. But their basic theory as to the nature of intelligence is such as to offer no sure foundation for the permanent victory of the cause they espoused. They resolved mind into a complex of external associations among atomic elements, just as they resolved society itself into a similar compound of external associations among individuals, each of whom has his own independently fixed nature. Their psychology was not in fact the product of impartial inquiry into human nature. It was rather a political weapon devised in the interest of breaking down the rigidity of dogmas and of institutions that had lost their relevancy. Mill's own contention that psychological laws of the kind he laid down were prior to the laws of men living and communicating together, acting and reacting upon one another, was itself a political instrument forged in the interest of criticism of beliefs and institutions that he believed should be displaced. The doctrine was potent in exposure of abuses; it was weak for constructive purposes. Bentham's assertion that he introduced the method of experiment into the social sciences held good as far as resolution into atoms acting externally upon one another, after the Newtonian model, was concerned. It did not recognize the place in experiment of comprehensive social ideas as working hypotheses in direction of action.

The practical consequence was also the logical one. When conditions had changed and the problem was one of constructing social organization from individual units that had been released from old social ties, liberalism fell upon evil times. The conception of intelligence as something that arose from the association of isolated elements, sensations and feelings, left no room for far-reaching experiments in construction of a new social order. It was definitely hostile to everything like collective social planning. The doctrine of *laissez faire* was applied to intelligence as well as to economic action, although the conception of experimental method in science demands a control by comprehensive ideas, projected in possibilities to be realized by action. Scientific method is as much opposed to go-as-you-please in intellectual matters as it is to reliance upon habits of mind whose sanction is that they were formed by ''experience'' in the past. The theory of mind held by the early liberals advanced beyond dependence upon the past but it did not arrive at the idea of experimental and constructive intelligence. . . .

The crisis in liberalism is connected with failure to develop and lay hold of an adequate conception of intelligence integrated with social movements and a factor in giving them direction. We cannot mete out harsh blame to the early liberals for failure to attain such a conception. The first scientific society for the study of anthropology was founded the year in which Darwin's *Origin of Species* saw the light of day. I cite this particular fact to typify the larger fact that the sciences of society, the controlled study of man in his relationships, are the product of the later nineteenth century. Moreover, these disciplines not only came into being too late to influence the formulation of liberal social theory, but they themselves were so much under the influence of the more advanced physical sciences that it was supposed that their findings were of merely theoretic import. By this statement, I mean that although the conclusions of the social disciplines were about man, they were treated as if they were of the same nature as the conclusions of physical science about remote galaxies of stars. Social and historical inquiry is in fact a part of the social process itself, not something outside of it. The consequence of not perceiving this fact was that the conclusions of the social sciences were not made (and still are not made in any large measure) integral members of a program of social action. When the conclusions of inquiries that deal with man are left outside the program of social action, social policies are necessarily left without the guidance that knowledge of man can provide, and that it must provide if social action is not to be directed either by mere precedent and custom or else by the happy intuitions of individual minds. The social conception of the nature and work of intelligence is still immature; in consequence, its use as a director of social action is inchoate and sporadic. It is the tragedy of earlier liberalism that just at the time when the problem of social organization was most urgent, liberals could bring to its solution nothing but the conception that intelligence is an individual possession. . . .

The inchoate state of social knowledge is reflected in the two fields where intelligence might be supposed to be most alert and most continuously active, education and the formation of social policies in legislation. Science is taught in our schools. But very largely it appears in schools simply as another study, to be acquired by much the same methods as are employed in "learning" the older studies that are part of the curriculum. If it were treated as what it is, the method of intelligence itself in action, then the method of science would be incarnate in every branch of study and every detail of learning. Thought would be connected with the possibility of action, and every mode of action would be reviewed to see its bearing upon the habits and ideas from which it sprang. Until science is treated educationally in this way, the introduction of what is called science into the schools signifies one more opportunity for the mechanization of the material and methods of study. When "learning" is treated not as an expansion of the understanding and judgment of meanings but as an acquisition of information, the method of coöperative experimental intelligence finds its way into the working structure of the individual only incidentally and by devious paths. . . .

. . . We are always dependent upon the experience that has accumulated in the past and yet there are always new forces coming in, new needs arising, that demand, if the new forces are to operate and the new needs to be satisfied, a reconstruction of the patterns of old experience. The old and the new have forever to be integrated with each other, so that the values of old experience may become the servants and instruments of new desires and aims. We are always possessed by habits and customs, and this fact signifies that we are always influenced by the inertia and the momentum of forces temporally outgrown but nevertheless still present with us as a part of our being. Human life gets set in patterns, institutional and moral. But change is also with us and demands the constant remaking of old habits and old ways of thinking, desiring and acting. The effective ratio between the old and the stabilizing and the new and disturbing is very different at different times. Sometimes whole communities seem to be dominated by custom, and changes are produced only by irruptions and invasions from outside. Sometimes, as at present, change is so varied and accelerated that customs seem to be dissolving before our very eyes. But be the ratio little or great, there is always an adjustment to be made, and as soon as the need for it becomes conscious, liberalism has a function and a meaning. It is not that liberalism creates the need, but that the necessity for adjustment defines the office of liberalism.

For the only adjustment that does not have to be made over again, and perhaps even under more unfavorable circumstances than when it was first attempted, is that effected through intelligence as a method. In its large sense, this remaking of the old through union with the new is precisely what intelligence is. It is conversion of past experience into knowledge and projection of that knowledge in ideas and purposes that anticipate what may come to be in the future and that indicate how to realize what is desired. Every problem that arises, personal or collective, simple or complex, is solved only by selecting material from the store of knowledge amassed in past experience and by bringing into play habits already formed. But the knowledge and the habits have to be modified to meet the new conditions that have arisen. In collective problems, the habits that are involved are traditions and institutions. The standing danger is either that they will be acted upon implicitly, without reconstruction to meet new conditions, or else that there will be an impatient and blind rush forward, directed only by some dogma rigidly adhered to. The office of intelligence in every problem that either a person or a community meets is to effect a working connection between old habits, customs, institutions, beliefs, and new conditions. What I have called the mediating function of liberalism is all one with the work of intelligence. This fact is the root, whether it be consciously realized or not, of the emphasis placed by liberalism upon the rôle of freed intelligence as the method of directing social action. . . .

The crisis in liberalism, as I said at the outset, proceeds from the fact that after early liberalism had done its work, society faced a new problem, that of social organization. Its work was to liberate a group of individuals, representing the new science and the new forces of productivity, from customs, ways of thinking, institutions, that were oppressive of the new modes of social action, however useful they may have been in their day. The instruments of analysis, of criticism, of dissolution, that were employed were effective for the work of release. But when it came to the problem of organizing the new forces and the individuals whose modes of life they radically altered into a coherent social organization, possessed of intellectual and moral directive power, liberalism was well-nigh impotent. The rise of national polities that pretend to represent the order, discipline and spiritual authority that will counteract social disintegration is a tragic comment upon the unpreparedness of older liberalism to deal with the new problem which its very success precipitated.

But the values of freed intelligence, of liberty, of opportunity for every individual to realize the potentialities of which he is possessed, are too precious to be sacrificed to a régime of despotism, especially when the régime is in such large measure merely the agent of a dominant economic class in its struggle to keep and extend the gains it has amassed at the expense of genuine social order, unity, and development. Liberalism has to gather itself together to formulate the ends to which it is devoted in terms of means that are relevant to the contemporary situation. . . .

Liberalism has to assume the responsibility for making it clear that intelligence is a social asset and is clothed with a function as public as is its origin, in the concrete, in social coöperation. It was

Comte who, in reaction against the purely individualistic ideas that seemed to him to underlie the French Revolution, said that in mathematics, physics and astronomy there is no right of private conscience. If we remove the statement from the context of actual scientific procedure, it is dangerous because it is false. The individual inquirer has not only the right but the duty to criticize the ideas, theories and "laws" that are current in science. But if we take the statement in the context of scientific method, it indicates that he carries on this criticism in virtue of a socially generated body of knowledge and by means of methods that are not of private origin and possession. He uses a method that retains public validity even when innovations are introduced in its use and application.

Henry George, speaking of ships that ply the ocean with a velocity of five or six hundred miles a day, remarked, "There is nothing whatever to show that the men who today build and navigate and use such ships are one whit superior in any physical or mental quality to their ancestors, whose best vessel was a coracle of wicker and hide. The enormous improvement which these ships show is not an improvement of human nature; it is an improvement of society—it is due to a wider and fuller union of individual efforts in accomplishment of common ends." This single instance, duly pondered, gives a better idea of the nature of intelligence and its social office than would a volume of abstract dissertation. Consider merely two of the factors that enter in and their social consequences. Consider what is involved in the production of steel, from the first use of fire and then the crude smelting of ore, to the processes that now effect the mass production of steel. Consider also the development of the power of guiding ships across trackless wastes from the day when they hugged the shore, steering by visible sun and stars, to the appliances that now enable a sure course to be taken. It would require a heavy tome to describe the advances in science, in mathematics, astronomy, physics, chemistry, that have made these two things possible. The record would be an account of a vast multitude of coöperative efforts, in which one individual uses the results provided for him by a countless number of other individuals, and uses them so as to add to the common and public store. A survey of such facts brings home the actual social character of intelligence as it actually develops and makes its way. . . .

It is to such things as these, rather than to abstract and formal psychology that we must go if we would learn the nature of intelligence: in itself, in its origin and development, and its uses and consequences. At this point, I should like to recur to an idea put forward in the preceding chapter. I then referred to the contempt often expressed for reliance upon intelligence as a social method, and I said this scorn is due to the identification of intelligence with native endowments of individuals. In contrast to this notion, I spoke of the power of individuals to appropriate and respond to the intelligence, the knowledge, ideas and purposes that have been integrated in the medium in which individuals live. Each of us knows, for example, some mechanic of ordinary native capacity who is intelligent within the matters of his calling. He has lived in an environment in which the cumulative intelligence of a multitude of coöperating individuals is embodied, and by the use of his native capacities he makes some phase of this intelligence his own. Given a social medium in whose institutions the available knowledge, ideas and art of humanity were incarnate, and the average individual would rise to undreamed heights of social and political intelligence.

The rub, the problem is found in the proviso. Can the intelligence actually existent and potentially available be embodied in that institutional medium in which an individual thinks, desires and acts? Before dealing directly with this question, I wish to say something about the operation of intelligence in our present political institutions, as exemplified by current practices of democratic government. I would not minimize the advance scored in substitution of methods of discussion and conference for the method of arbitrary rule. But the better is too often the enemy of the still better. Discussion, as the manifestation of intelligence in political life, stimulates publicity; by its means sore spots are brought to light that would otherwise remain hidden. It affords opportunity for promulgation of new ideas. Compared with despotic rule, it is an invitation to individuals to concern themselves with public affairs. But discussion and dialectic, however indispensable they are to the elaboration of ideas and policies after ideas are once put forth, are weak reeds to depend upon for systematic origination of comprehensive plans, the plans that are required if the problem of social organization is to be met. There was a time when discussion, the comparison of ideas already current so as to purify and clarify them, was thought to be sufficient in discovery of the structure and laws of physical nature. In the latter field, the method was displaced by that of experimental observation guided by comprehensive working hypotheses, and using all the resources made available by mathematics.

But we still depend upon the method of discussion, with only incidental scientific control, in politics. Our system of popular suffrage, immensely valuable as it is in comparison with what preceded it, exhibits the idea that intelligence is an individualistic possession, at best enlarged by public discussion. Existing political practice, with its complete ignoring of occupational groups and the organized knowledge and purposes that are involved in the existence of such groups, manifests a dependence upon a summation of individuals quantitatively, similar to Bentham's purely quantitative formula of the greatest sum of pleasures of the greatest possible number. The formation of parties or, as the eighteenth-century writers called them, factions, and the system of party government is the practically necessary counterweight to a numerical and atomistic individualism. The idea that the conflict of parties will, by means of public discussion, bring out necessary public truths is a kind of political watered-down version of the Hegelian dialectic, with its synthesis arrived at by a union of antithetical conceptions. The method has nothing in common with the procedure of organized coöperative inquiry which has won the triumphs of science in the field of physical nature. . . .

. . . The crisis in democracy demands the substitution of the intelligence that is exemplified in scientific procedure for the kind of intelligence that is now accepted. The need for this change is not exhausted in the demand for greater honesty and impartiality, even though these qualities be now corrupted by discussion carried on mainly for purposes of party supremacy and for imposition of some special but concealed interest. These qualities need to be restored. But the need goes further. The social use of intelligence would remain deficient even if these moral traits were exalted, and yet intelligence continued to be identified simply with discussion and persuasion, necessary as are these things. Approximation to use of scientific method in investigation and of the engineering mind in the invention and projection of far-reaching social plans is demanded. The habit of considering social realities in terms of cause and effect and social policies in terms of means and consequences is still inchoate. The contrast between the state of intelligence in politics and in the physical control of nature is to be taken literally. What has happened in this latter is the outstanding demonstration of the meaning of organized intelligence. The combined effect of science and technology has released more productive energies in a bare hundred years than stands to the credit of prior human history in its entirety. Productively it has multiplied nine million times in the last generation alone. The prophetic vision of Francis Bacon of subjugation of the energies of nature through change in methods of inquiry has well-nigh been realized. The stationary engine, the locomotive, the dynamo, the motor car, turbine, telegraph, telephone, radio and moving picture are not the product of either isolated individual minds nor of the particular economic régime called capitalism. They are the fruit of methods that first penetrated to the working causalities of nature and then utilized the resulting knowledge in bold imaginative ventures of invention and construction. . . .

It is frequently asserted that the method of experimental intelligence can be applied to physical facts because physical nature does not present conflicts of class interests, while it is inapplicable to society because the latter is so deeply marked by incompatible interests. It is then assumed that the "experimentalist" is one who has chosen to ignore the uncomfortable fact of conflicting interests. Of course, there *are* conflicting interests; otherwise there would be no social problems. The problem under discussion is precisely *how* conflicting claims are to be settled in the interest of the widest possible contribution to the interests of all—or at least of the great majority. The method of democracy—inasfar as it is that of organized intelligence—is to bring these conflicts out into the open where their special claims can be seen and appraised, where they can be discussed and judged in the light of more inclusive interests than are represented by either of them separately. . . .

It would be fantastic folly to ignore or to belittle the obstacles that stand in the way. But what has taken place, also against great odds, in the scientific and industrial revolutions, is an accomplished fact; the way is marked out. It may be that the way will remain untrodden. If so, the future holds the menace of confusion moving into chaos, a chaos that will be externally masked for a time by an organization of force, coercive and violent, in which the liberties of men will all but disappear. Even so, the cause of the liberty of the human spirit, the cause of opportunity of human beings for full development of their powers, the cause for which liberalism enduringly stands, is too precious and too ingrained in the human constitution to be forever obscured. Intelligence after millions of years of errancy has found itself as a method, and it will not be lost forever in the blackness of night. The business of liberalism is to bend every energy and exhibit every courage so that these precious goods may not even be temporarily lost but be intensified and expanded here and now.

5. THE DEMOCRATIC PUBLIC

In the passages below from The Public and Its Problems, *Dewey identifies some of the principal conditions that must be satisfied if a genuinely democratic public is to emerge.*[4] *He does not use 'public' in the usual vague sense; it is a more specific and operational concept. In Dewey's sense, a public*

originates from any group of people whose lives are significantly affected by
the behavior of other groups, whether the effects are deliberate or not. The ac-
tivities of economic interests, for example, may be intended for private profit;
but they also have extensive and enduring consequences for others. These
others constitute a public only when they recognize themselves as such—only
when they have some shared and explicit understanding of their situation. At
that point they are for the first time a public in Dewey's sense. When certain
further conditions are fulfilled, they will be prepared for effective participation
in democratic action.

    . . . Indirect, extensive, enduring and serious consequences of
conjoint and interacting behavior call a public into existence having a
common interest in controlling these consequences. But the machine
age has so enormously expanded, multiplied, intensified and complicated the scope of the indirect consequences, has formed such immense and consolidated unions in action, on an impersonal rather
than a community basis, that the resultant public cannot identify and
distinguish itself. And this discovery is obviously an antecedent condition of any effective organization on its part. Such is our thesis
regarding the eclipse which the public idea and interest have under-
gone. There are too many publics and too much of public concern for
our existing resources to cope with. The problem of a democratically
organized public is primarily and essentially an intellectual problem,
in a degree to which the political affairs of prior ages offer no
parallel. . . .

    . . . The local face-to-face community has been invaded by forces
so vast, so remote in initiation, so far-reaching in scope and so complexly indirect in operation, that they are, from the standpoint of the
members of local social units, unknown. Man, as has been often
remarked, has difficulty in getting on either with or without his fel-
lows, even in neighborhoods. He is not more successful in getting
on with them when they act at a great distance in ways invisible to
him. An inchoate public is capable of organization only when indirect
consequences are perceived, and when it is possible to project agencies which order their occurrence. At present, many consequences
are felt rather than perceived; they are suffered, but they cannot be
said to be known, for they are not, by those who experience them,
referred to their origins. It goes, then, without saying that agencies
are not established which canalize the streams of social action and
thereby regulate them. Hence the publics are amorphous and unar-
ticulated.

    There was a time when a man might entertain a few general

political principles and apply them with some confidence. A citizen believed in states' rights or in a centralized federal government; in free trade or protection. It did not involve much mental strain to imagine that by throwing in his lot with one party or another he could so express his views that his belief would count in government. For the average voter to-day the tariff question is a complicated medley of infinite detail, schedules of rates specific and *ad valorem* on countless things, many of which he does not recognize by name, and with respect to which he can form no judgment. Probably not one voter in a thousand even reads the scores of pages in which the rates of toll are enumerated and he would not be much wiser if he did. The average man gives it up as a bad job. At election time, appeal to some time-worn slogan may galvanize him into a temporary notion that he has convictions on an important subject, but except for manufacturers and dealers who have some interest at stake in this or that schedule, belief lacks the qualities which attach to beliefs about matters of personal concern. Industry is too complex and intricate. . . .

Political apathy, which is a natural product of the discrepancies between actual practices and traditional machinery, ensues from inability to identify one's self with definite issues. These are hard to find and locate in the vast complexities of current life. When traditional war-cries have lost their import in practical policies which are consonant with them, they are readily dismissed as bunk. Only habit and tradition, rather than reasoned conviction, together with a vague faith in doing one's civic duty, send to the polls a considerable percentage of the fifty per cent who still vote. And of them it is a common remark that a large number vote against something or somebody rather than for anything or anybody, except when powerful agencies create a scare. The old principles do not fit contemporary life as it is lived, however well they may have expressed the vital interests of the times in which they arose. Thousands feel their hollowness even if they cannot make their feeling articulate. The confusion which has resulted from the size and ramifications of social activities has rendered men skeptical of the efficiency of political action. Who is sufficient unto these things? Men feel that they are caught in the sweep of forces too vast to understand or master. Thought is brought to a standstill and action paralyzed. Even the specialist finds it difficult to trace the chain of "cause and effect"; and even he operates only after the event, looking backward, while meantime social activities have moved on to effect a new state of affairs. . . .

. . . Conditions have changed, but every aspect of life, from religion and education to property and trade, shows that nothing approaching a transformation has taken place in ideas and ideals. Symbols control sentiment and thought, and the new age has no symbols consonant with its activities. Intellectual instrumentalities for the formation of an organized public are more inadequate than its overt means. The ties which hold men together in action are numerous, tough and subtle. But they are invisible and intangible. We have the physical tools of communication as never before. The thoughts and aspirations congruous with them are not communicated, and hence are not common. Without such communication the public will remain shadowy and formless, seeking spasmodically for itself, but seizing and holding its shadow rather than its substance. Till the Great Society is converted into a Great Community, the Public will remain in eclipse. Communication can alone create a great community. Our Babel is not one of tongues but of the signs and symbols without which shared experience is impossible. . . .

. . . What are the conditions under which it is possible for the Great Society to approach more closely and vitally the status of a Great Community, and thus take form in genuinely democratic societies and state? What are the conditions under which we may reasonably picture the Public emerging from its eclipse?

The study will be an intellectual or hypothetical one. There will be no attempt to state how the required conditions might come into existence, nor to prophesy that they will occur. The object of the analysis will be to show that *unless* ascertained specifications are realized, the Community cannot be organized as a democratically effective Public. It is not claimed that the conditions which will be noted will suffice, but only that at least they are indispensable. In other words, we shall endeavor to frame a hypothesis regarding the democratic state to stand in contrast with the earlier doctrine which has been nullified by the course of events.

Two essential constituents in that older theory, as will be recalled, were the notions that each individual is of himself equipped with the intelligence needed, under the operation of self-interest, to engage in political affairs; and that general suffrage, frequent elections of officials and majority rule are sufficient to ensure the responsibility of elected rulers to the desires and interests of the public. As we shall see, the second conception is logically bound up with the first and stands or falls with it. At the basis of the scheme lies what Lippmann has well called the idea of the "omnicompetent" individual: competent to frame policies, to judge their results; competent to know in all situations demanding political action what is for his own good, and competent to enforce his idea of good and the will to effect it against contrary forces. Subsequent history has proved that the assumption involved illusion. Had it not been for the misleading influence of a false psychology, the illusion might have been detected in advance. But current philosophy held that ideas and knowledge were functions of a mind or consciousness which originated in individuals by means of isolated contact with objects. But in fact, knowledge is a function of association and communication; it depends upon tradition, upon tools and methods socially transmitted, developed and sanctioned. Faculties of effectual observation, reflection and desire are habits acquired under the influence of the culture and institutions of society, not ready-made inherent powers. The fact that man acts from crudely intelligized emotion and from habit rather than from rational consideration, is now so familiar that it is not easy to appreciate that the other idea was taken seriously as the basis of economic and political philosophy. . . .

Dewey's reference to habit in the sentences just above is to blind or routine habit. He goes on to say that even rationality is a habit; it is achieved only as the circumstances of one's environment are such as to form and nourish habits of intelligent inquiry and participation. Hence we should not prematurely despair for democracy. Irrationality in individuals does not reflect native incompetence, but failure in education. Just because of the strength of habit, however, deliberate change is very difficult to accomplish.

Habit is the mainspring of human action, and habits are formed for the most part under the influence of the customs of a group. . . .

The influence of habit is decisive because all distinctively human action has to be learned, and the very heart, blood and sinews of learning is creation of habitudes. Habits bind us to orderly and established ways of action because they generate ease, skill and interest in things to which we have grown used and because they instigate fear to walk in different ways, and because they leave us incapacitated for the trial of them. Habit does not preclude the use of thought, but it determines the channels within which it operates. Thinking is secreted in the interstices of habits. The sailor, miner, fisherman and farmer think, but their thoughts fall within the framework of accustomed occupations and relationships. We dream beyond the limits of use and wont, but only rarely does revery become a source of acts which break bounds; so rarely that we name those in whom it happens demonic geniuses and marvel at the spectacle. Thinking itself becomes habitual along certain lines; a specialized occupation. Scientific men, philosophers, literary persons, are not men and women who have so broken the bonds of habits that pure reason and emotion undefiled by use and wont speak through them. They are persons of a specialized infrequent habit. Hence the idea that men are moved by an intelligent and calculated regard for their own good is pure mythology. Even if the principle of self-love actuated behavior, it would still be true that the *objects* in which men find their love manifested, the objects which they take as constituting their peculiar interests, are set by habits reflecting social customs. . . .

. . . Not only are personal desire and belief functions of habit and custom, but the objective conditions which provide the resources and tools of action, together with its limitations, obstructions and traps, are precipitates of the past, perpetuating, willy-nilly, its hold and power. The creation of a *tabula rasa* in order to permit the creation of a new order is so impossible as to set at naught both the hope of buoyant revolutionaries and the timidity of scared conservatives. . . .

. . . The prime condition of a democratically organized public is a kind of knowledge and insight which does not yet exist. In its absence, it would be the height of absurdity to try to tell what it would be like if it existed. But some of the conditions which must be fulfilled if it is to exist can be indicated. We can borrow that much from the spirit and method of science even if we are ignorant of it as a specialized apparatus. An obvious requirement is freedom of social inquiry and of distribution of its conclusions. The notion that men may be free in their thought even when they are not in its expression and dissemination has been sedulously propagated. It had its origin in the idea of a mind complete in itself, apart from action and from objects. Such a consciousness presents in fact the spectacle of mind deprived of its normal functioning, because it is baffled by the actualities in connection with which alone it is truly mind, and is driven back into secluded and impotent revery.

There can be no public without full publicity in respect to all consequences which concern it. Whatever obstructs and restricts publicity, limits and distorts public opinion and checks and distorts thinking on social affairs. Without freedom of expression, not even methods of social inquiry can be developed. For tools can be evolved and perfected only in operation; in application to observing, reporting and organizing actual subject-matter; and this application cannot occur save through free and systematic communication. The early history of physical knowledge, of Greek conceptions of natural phenomena, proves how inept become the conceptions of the best endowed minds when those ideas are elaborated apart from the closest contact with the events which they purport to state and explain. The ruling ideas and methods of the human sciences are in much the same condition to-day. They are also evolved on the basis of past gross observations, remote from constant use in regulation of the material of new observations.

The belief that thought and its communication are now free simply because legal restrictions which once obtained have been done away with is absurd. Its currency perpetuates the infantile state of social knowledge. For it blurs recognition of our central need to possess conceptions which are used as tools of directed inquiry and which are tested, rectified and caused to grow in actual use. No man and no mind was ever emancipated merely by being left alone. Removal of formal limitations is but a negative condition; positive freedom is not a state but an act which involves methods and instrumentalities for control of conditions. Experience shows that sometimes the sense of external oppression, as by censorship, acts as a challenge and arouses intellectual energy and excites courage. But a belief in intellectual freedom where it does not exist contributes only to complacency in virtual enslavement, to sloppiness, superficiality and recourse to sensations as a substitute for ideas: marked traits of our present estate with respect to social knowledge. On one hand, thinking deprived of its normal course takes refuge in academic specialism, comparable in its way to what is called scholasticism. On the other hand, the physical agencies of publicity which exist in such abundance are utilized in ways which constitute a large part of the present meaning of publicity: advertising, propaganda, invasion of private life, the "featuring" of passing incidents in a way which violates all the moving logic of continuity, and which leaves us with those isolated intrusions and shocks which are the essence of "sensations."

It would be a mistake to identify the conditions which limit free communication and circulation of facts and ideas, and which thereby arrest and pervert social thought or inquiry, merely with overt forces which are obstructive. It is true that those who have ability to manipulate social relations for their own advantage have to be reckoned with. They have an uncanny instinct for detecting whatever intellectual tendencies even remotely threaten to encroach upon their control. They have developed an extraordinary facility in enlisting upon their side the inertia, prejudices and emotional partisanship of the masses by use of a technique which impedes free inquiry and expression. We seem to be approaching a state of government by hired promoters of opinion called publicity agents. But the more serious enemy is deeply concealed in hidden entrenchments.

Emotional habituations and intellectual habitudes on the part of the mass of men create the conditions of which the exploiters of sentiment and opinion only take advantage. Men have got used to an experimental method in physical and technical matters. They are still afraid of it in human concerns. . . .

It has been implied throughout that knowledge is communication as well as understanding. I well remember the saying of a man, un-educated from the standpoint of the schools, in speaking of certain mat-ters: "Sometime they will be found out and not only found out, but they will be known." The schools may suppose that a thing is known when it is found out. My old friend was aware that a thing is fully known only when it is published, shared, socially accessible. Record and com-munication are indispensable to knowledge. Knowledge cooped up in a private consciousness is a myth, and knowledge of social phenomena is peculiarly dependent upon dissemination, for only by distribution can such knowledge be either obtained or tested. A fact of community life which is not spread abroad so as to be a common possession is a contradiction in terms. Dissemination is something other than scatter-ing at large. Seeds are sown, not by virtue of being thrown out at ran-dom, but by being so distributed as to take root and have a chance of growth. Communication of the results of social inquiry is the same thing as the formation of public opinion. This marks one of the first ideas framed in the growth of political democracy as it will be one of the last to be fulfilled. For public opinion is judgment which is formed and entertained by those who constitute the public and is about public affairs. Each of the two phases imposes for its realization conditions hard to meet.

Opinions and beliefs concerning the public presuppose effective and organized inquiry. Unless there are methods for detecting the energies which are at work and tracing them through an intricate net-work of interactions to their consequences, what passes as public opinion will be "opinion" in its derogatory sense rather than truly public, no matter how widespread the opinion is. The number who share error as to fact and who partake of a false belief measures power for harm. Opinion casually formed and formed under the direction of those who have something at stake in having a lie believed can be *public* opinion only in name. Calling it by this name, acceptance of the name as a kind of warrant, magnifies its capacity to lead action estray. The more who share it, the more injurious its influence. . . .

There is a sense in which "opinion" rather than knowledge, even under the most favorable circumstances, is the proper term to use—namely, in the sense of judgment, estimate. For in its strict sense, knowledge can refer only to what *has* happened and been done. What is still *to be* done involves a forecast of a future still contingent, and cannot escape the liability to error in judgment involved in all an-ticipation of probabilities. There may well be honest divergence as to policies to be pursued, even when plans spring from knowledge of the same facts. But genuinely public policy cannot be generated unless it be informed by knowledge, and this knowledge does not exist except when there is systematic, thorough, and well-equipped search and record.

Moreover, inquiry must be as nearly contemporaneous as possible; otherwise it is only of antiquarian interest. Knowledge of history is evidently necessary for connectedness of knowledge. But history which is not brought down close to the actual scene of events leaves a gap and exercises influence upon the formation of judgments about the public interest only by guess-work about intervening events. Here, only too conspicuously, is a limitation of the existing social sciences. Their material comes too late, too far after the event, to enter effectively into the formation of public opinion about the immediate public concern and what is to be done about it.

A glance at the situation shows that the physical and external means of collecting information in regard to what is happening in the world have far outrun the intellectual phase of inquiry and organization of its results. Telegraph, telephone, and now the radio, cheap and quick mails, the printing press, capable of swift reduplication of material at low cost, have attained a remarkable development. But when we ask what sort of material is recorded and how it is organized, when we ask about the intellectual form in which the material is presented, the tale to be told is very different. "News" signifies something which has just happened, and which is new just because it deviates from the old and regular. But its *meaning* depends upon relation to what it imports, to what its social consequences are. This import cannot be determined unless the new is placed in relation to the old, to what has happened and been integrated into the course of events. Without coordination and consecutiveness, events are not events, but mere occurrences, intrusions; an event implies that out of which a happening proceeds. Hence even if we discount the influence of private interests in procuring suppression, secrecy and misrepresentation, we have here an explanation of the triviality and "sensational" quality of so much of what passes as news. The catastrophic, namely, crime, accident, family rows, personal clashes and conflicts, are the most obvious forms of breaches of continuity; they supply the element of shock which is the strictest meaning of sensation; they are the *new* par excellence, even though only the date of the newspaper could inform us whether they happened last year or this, so completely are they isolated from their connections.

So accustomed are we to this method of collecting, recording and presenting social changes, that it may well sound ridiculous to say that a genuine social science would manifest its reality in the daily press, while learned books and articles supply and polish tools of inquiry. But the inquiry which alone can furnish knowledge as a precondition of public judgments must be contemporary and quotidian. Even if social sciences as a specialized apparatus of inquiry were more advanced than they are, they would be comparatively impotent in the office of directing opinion on matters of concern to the public as long as they are remote from application in the daily and unremitting assembly and interpretation of "news." On the other hand, the tools of social inquiry will be clumsy as long as they are forged in places and under conditions remote from contemporary events. . . .

One aspect of the matter concerns particularly the side of dissemination. It is often said, and with a great appearance of truth, that the freeing and perfecting of inquiry would not have any especial effect. For, it is argued, the mass of the reading public is not interested in learning and assimilating the results of accurate investigation. Unless these are read, they cannot seriously affect the thought and action of members of the public; they remain in secluded library alcoves, and are studied and understood only by a few intellectuals. The objection is well taken save as the potency of art is taken into account. A technical high-brow presentation would appeal only to those technically highbrow; it would not be news to the masses. Presentation is fundamentally important, and presentation is a question of art. A newspaper which was only a daily edition of a quarterly journal of sociology or political science would undoubtedly possess a limited circulation and a narrow influence. Even at that, however, the mere existence and accessibility of such material would have some regulative effect. But we can look much further than that. The material would have such an enormous and widespread human bearing that its bare existence would be an irresistible invitation to a presentation of it which would have a direct popular appeal. The freeing of the artist in literary presentation, in other words, is as much a precondition of the desirable creation of adequate opinion on public matters as is the freeing of social inquiry. Men's conscious life of opinion and judgment often proceeds on a superficial and trivial plane. But their lives reach a deeper level. The function of art has always been to break through the crust of conventionalized and routine consciousness. Common things, a flower, a gleam of moonlight, the song of a bird, not things rare and remote, are means with which the deeper levels of life are touched so that they spring up as desire and thought. This process is art. Poetry, the drama, the novel, are proofs that the problem of presentation is not insoluble. Artists have always been the real purveyors of news, for it is not the outward happening in itself which is new, but the kindling by it of emotion, perception and appreciation. . . .

. . . The highest and most difficult kind of inquiry and a subtle, delicate, vivid and responsive art of communication must take possession of the physical machinery of transmission and circulation and breathe life into it. When the machine age has thus perfected its machinery it will be a means of life and not its despotic master. Democracy will come into its own, for democracy is a name for a life of free and enriching communion. It had its seer in Walt Whitman. It will have its consummation when free social inquiry is indissolubly wedded to the art of full and moving communication. . . .

These considerations suggest a brief discussion of the effect of the present absolutistic logic upon the method and aims of education, not just in the sense of schooling but with respect to all the ways in which communities attempt to shape the disposition and beliefs of their members. Even when the processes of education do not aim at the unchanged perpetuation of existing institutions, it is assumed that there must be a mental picture of some desired end, personal and social, which is to be attained, and that this conception of a fixed determinate end ought to control educative processes. Reformers share this conviction with conservatives. The disciples of Lenin and Mussolini vie with the captains of capitalistic society in endeavoring to bring about a formation of dispositions and ideas which will conduce to a preconceived goal. If there is a difference, it is that the former proceed more consciously. An experimental social method would probably manifest itself first of all in surrender of this notion. Every care would be taken to surround the young with the physical and social conditions which best conduce, as far as freed knowledge extends, to release of personal potentialities. The habits thus formed would have entrusted to them the meeting of future social requirements and the development of the future state of society. Then and then only would all social agencies that are available operate as resources in behalf of a bettered community life. . . .

The essential need, in other words, is the improvement of the methods and conditions of debate, discussion and persuasion. That is *the* problem of the public. We have asserted that this improvement depends essentially upon freeing and perfecting the processes of inquiry and of dissemination of their conclusions. Inquiry, indeed, is a work which devolves upon experts. But their expertness is not shown in framing and executing policies, but in discovering and making known the facts upon which the former depend. They are technical experts in the sense that scientific investigators and artists manifest *expertise.*

It is not necessary that the many should have the knowledge and skill to carry on the needed investigations; what is required is that they have the ability to judge of the bearing of the knowledge supplied by others upon common concerns.

It is easy to exaggerate the amount of intelligence and ability demanded to render such judgments fitted for their purpose. In the first place, we are likely to form our estimate on the basis of present conditions. But indubitably one great trouble at present is that the data for good judgment are lacking; and no innate faculty of mind can make up for the absence of facts. Until secrecy, prejudice, bias, misrepresentation, and propaganda as well as sheer ignorance are replaced by inquiry and publicity, we have no way of telling how apt for judgment of social policies the existing intelligence of the masses may be. It would certainly go much further than at present. In the second place, *effective* intelligence is not an original, innate endowment. No matter what are the differences in native intelligence (allowing for the moment that intelligence can be native), the actuality of mind is dependent upon the education which social conditions effect. Just as the specialized mind and knowledge of the past is embodied in implements, utensils, devices and technologies which those of a grade of intelligence which could not produce them can now intelligently use, so it will be when currents of public knowledge blow through social affairs. . . .

. . . A more intelligent state of social affairs, one more informed with knowledge, more directed by intelligence, would not improve original endowments one whit, but it would raise the level upon which the intelligence of all operates. The height of this level is much more important for judgment of public concerns than are differences in intelligence quotients. . . .

A point which concerns us in conclusion passes beyond the field of intellectual method, and trenches upon the question of practical reformation of social conditions. In its deepest and richest sense a community must always remain a matter of face-to-face intercourse. This is why the family and neighborhood, with all their deficiencies, have always been the chief agencies of nurture, the means by which dispositions are stably formed and ideas acquired which laid hold on the roots of character. The Great Community, in the sense of free and full intercommunication, is conceivable. But it can never possess all the qualities which mark a local community. It will do its final work in ordering the relations and enriching the experience of local associations. The invasion and partial destruction of the life of the latter by outside uncontrolled agencies is the immediate source of the instability, disintegration and restlessness which characterize the present epoch. Evils which are uncritically and indiscriminately laid at the door of industrialism and democracy might, with greater intelligence, be referred to the dislocation and unsettlement of local communities. Vital and thorough attachments are bred only in the intimacy of an intercourse which is of necessity restricted in range.

Is it possible for local communities to be stable without being static, progressive without being merely mobile? Can the vast, innumerable and intricate currents of trans-local associations be so banked and conducted that they will pour the generous and abundant meanings of which they are potential bearers into the smaller intimate únions of human beings living in immediate contact with one another? Is it possible to restore the reality of the lesser communal organizations and to penetrate and saturate their members with a sense of local community life? There is at present, at least in theory, a movement away from the principle of territorial organization to that of ''functional,'' that is to say, occupational, organization. It is true enough that older forms of territorial association do not satisfy present needs. It is true that ties formed by sharing in common work, whether in what is called industry or what are called professions, have now a force which formerly they did not possess. But these ties can be counted upon for an enduring and stable organization, which at the same time is flexible and moving, only as they grow out of immediate intercourse and attachment. The theory, as far as it relies upon associations which are remote and indirect, would if carried into effect soon be confronted by all the troubles and evils of the present situation in a transposed form. There is no substitute for the vitality and depth of close and direct intercourse and attachment.

It is said, and said truly, that for the world's peace it is necessary that we understand the peoples of foreign lands. How well do we understand, I wonder, our next door neighbors? It has also been said that if a man love not his fellow man whom he has seen, he cannot love the God whom he has not seen. The chances of regard for distant peoples being effective as long as there is no close neighborhood experience to bring with it insight and understanding of neighbors do not seem better. A man who has not been seen in the daily relations of life may inspire admiration, emulation, servile subjection, fanatical partisanship, hero worship; but not love and understanding, save as they radiate from the attachments of a near-by union. Democracy must begin at home, and its home is the neighborly community. . . .

We have said that consideration of this particular condition of the generation of democratic communities and an articulate democratic public carries us beyond the question of intellectual method into that of practical procedure. But the two questions are not disconnected.

The problem of securing diffused and seminal intelligence can be solved only in the degree in which local communal life becomes a reality. Signs and symbols, language, are the means of communication by which a fraternally shared experience is ushered in and sustained. But the wingèd words of conversation in immediate intercourse have a vital import lacking in the fixed and frozen words of written speech. Systematic and continuous inquiry into all the conditions which affect association and their dissemination in print is a precondition of the creation of a true public. But it and its results are but tools after all. Their final actuality is accomplished in face-to-face relations by means of direct give and take. Logic in its fulfillment recurs to the primitive sense of the word: dialogue. Ideas which are not communicated, shared, and reborn in expression are but soliloquy, and soliloquy is but broken and imperfect thought. It, like the acquisition of material wealth, marks a diversion of the wealth created by associated endeavor and exchange to private ends. It is more genteel, and it is called more noble. But there is no difference in kind.

In a word, that expansion and reenforcement of personal understanding and judgment by the cumulative and transmitted intellectual wealth of the community which may render nugatory the indictment of democracy drawn on the basis of the ignorance, bias and levity of the masses, can be fulfilled only in the relations of personal intercourse in the local community. The connections of the ear with vital and outgoing thought and emotion are immensely closer and more varied than those of the eye. Vision is a spectator; hearing is a participator. Publication is partial and the public which results is partially informed and formed until the meanings it purveys pass from mouth to mouth. There is no limit to the liberal expansion and confirmation of limited personal intellectual endowment which may proceed from the flow of social intelligence when that circulates by word of mouth from one to another in the communications of the local community. That and that only gives reality to public opinion. We lie, as Emerson said, in the lap of an immense intelligence. But that intelligence is dormant and its communications are broken, inarticulate and faint until it possesses the local community as its medium.

6. EXPERIMENTALISM AND DOGMATISM

The following paragraphs from the Ethics *provide a brief statement advocating democratic method in social decision making, in contrast to dogmatic method.*[5]

. . . The controversy between believers in private and in public action is manifested in every issue which concerns the extent and area of governmental action. . . .

The attempt to settle these issues in our discussion of ethics would obviously involve an exhibition of partisanship. But, what is more important, it would involve the adoption of a method which has been expressly criticized and repudiated. It would assume the existence of final and unquestionable knowledge upon which we can fall back in order to settle automatically every moral problem. It would involve the commitment to a dogmatic theory of morals. The alternative method may be called experimental. It implies that reflective morality demands observation of particular situations, rather than fixed adherence to *a priori* principles; that free inquiry and freedom of publication and discussion must be encouraged and not merely grudgingly tolerated; that opportunity at different times and places must be given for trying different measures so that their effects may be capable of observation and of comparison with one another. It is, in short, the method of democracy, of a positive toleration which amounts to sympathetic regard for the intelligence and personality of others, even if they hold views opposed to ours, and of scientific inquiry into facts and testing of ideas.

The opposed method, even when we free it from the extreme traits of forcible suppression, censorship, and intolerant persecution which have often historically accompanied it, is the method of appeal to authority and to precedent. The will of divine beings, supernaturally revealed; of divinely ordained rulers; of so-called natural law, philosophically interpreted; of private conscience; of the commands of the state, or the constitution; of common consent; of a majority; of received conventions; of traditions coming from a hoary past; of the wisdom of ancestors; of precedents set up in the past, have at different times been the authority appealed to. The common feature of the appeal is that there is some voice so authoritative as to preclude the need of inquiry. The logic of the various positions is that while an open mind may be desirable in respect to physical truths, a completely settled and closed mind is needed in moral matters.

Adoption of the experimental method does not signify that there is no place for authority and precedent. On the contrary, precedent is, as we noted in another connection, a valuable *instrumentality*. . . . But precedents are to be *used* rather than to be implicitly followed; they are to be used as tools of analysis of present situations, suggesting points to be looked into and hypotheses to be tried. . . .

To some persons it may seem an academic matter whether their attitude and the method they follow in judging the ethical values of social institutions, customs, and traditions, be experimental or dogmatic and closed; whether they proceed by study of consequences, of the working of condition, or by an attempt to dispose of all questions by reference to preformed absolute standards. There is, however, no opening for application of scientific method in social morals unless the former procedure is adopted. There is at least a presumption that the development of methods of objective and impartial inquiry in social affairs would be as significant there as it has proved in physical matters. The alternative to organic inquiry is reliance upon prejudice, partisanship, upon tradition accepted without questioning, upon the varying pressures of immediate circumstance. Adoption of an experimental course of judgment would work virtually a moral revolution in social judgments and practice. It would eliminate the chief causes of intolerance, persecution, fanaticism, and the use of differences of opinion to create class wars. It is for such reasons as these that it is claimed that, at the present time, the question of method to be used in judging existing customs and policies proposed is of greater moral significance than the particular conclusion reached in connection with any one controversy.

7. DEMOCRACY AS A WAY OF LIFE

The last selection, provided in its entirety, is ''Creative Democracy—The Task Before Us'' (1940). If we were to make some approximation to the democratic ethos outlined in this essay, we might be equal to the problems that beset us. In contrast to Dewey's ethic, the cries of those who say the moral life is a shambles without moral absolutes are unconvincing. The absolutists crave exactitude and certitude. Both of these are impossible, however; and the pretenders to such verities tend to duel with each other to the death over them. If we possessed even a significant measure of the moral and intellectual virtues organic to the democratic ideal, we would not eliminate uncertainty about many of our decisions; and we would not eliminate conflict and controversy. Yet this condition would be far removed from moral chaos. We must distinguish individuals of democratic virtue not only from absolutists, but also from murderers, liars, bigots, thieves, terrorists—corrupt and anti-social types of every description. Persons living by the democratic guide are better suited to attain moral harmony and fulfillment than either those who are devoted to the quest for certainty or those who would be parasites or oppressors.

Under present circumstances I cannot hope to conceal the fact that I have managed to exist eighty years. Mention of the fact may suggest to you a more important fact—namely, that events of the utmost significance for the destiny of this country have taken place during the past four-fifths of a century, a period that covers more than half of its national life in its present form. For obvious reasons I shall not attempt a summary of even the more important of these events. I refer here to them because of their bearing upon the issue to which this country committed itself when the nation took shape—the creation of democracy, an issue which is now as urgent as it was a hundred and fifty years ago when the most experienced and wisest men of the country gathered to take stock of conditions and to create the political structure of a self-governing society.

For the net import of the changes that have taken place in these later years is that ways of life and institutions which were once the natural, almost the inevitable, product of fortunate conditions have now to be won by conscious and resolute effort. Not all the country was in a pioneer state eighty years ago. But it was still, save perhaps in a few large cities, so close to the pioneer stage of American life that the traditions of the pioneer, indeed of the frontier, were active agencies in forming the thoughts and shaping the beliefs of those who were born into its life. In imagination at least the country was still having an open frontier, one of unused and unappropriated resources. It was a country of physical opportunity and invitation. Even so, there was more than a marvelous conjunction of physical circumstances involved in bringing to birth this new nation. There was in existence a group of men who were capable of readapting older institutions and ideas to meet the situations provided by new physical conditions—a group of men extraordinarily gifted in political inventiveness.

At the present time, the frontier is moral, not physical. The period of free lands that seemed boundless in extent has vanished. Unused resources are now human rather than material. They are found in the waste of grown men and women who are without the chance to work, and in the young men and young women who find doors closed where there was once opportunity. The crisis that one hundred and fifty years ago called out social and political inventiveness is with us in a form which puts a heavier demand on human creativeness.

At all events this is what I mean when I say that we now have to re-create by deliberate and determined endeavor the kind of democracy which in its origin one hundred and fifty years ago was largely the product of a fortunate combination of men and circumstances. We have lived for a long time upon the heritage that came to us from the happy conjunction of men and events in an earlier day. The present state of the world is more than a reminder that we have now to put forth every energy of our own to prove worthy of our heritage. It is a challenge to do for the critical and complex conditions of today what the men of an earlier day did for simpler conditions.

If I emphasize that the task can be accomplished only by inventive effort and creative activity, it is in part because the depth of the present crisis is due in considerable part to the fact that for a long period we acted as if our democracy were something that perpetuated itself automatically; as if our ancestors had succeeded in setting up a machine that solved the problem of perpetual motion in politics. We acted as if democracy were something that took place mainly at Washington and Albany—or some other state capital—under the impetus of what happened when men and women went to the polls once a year or so—which is a somewhat extreme way of saying that we have had the habit of thinking of democracy as a kind of political mechanism that will work as long as citizens were reasonably faithful in performing political duties.

Of late years we have heard more and more frequently that this is not enough; that democracy is a way of life. This saying gets down to hard pan. But I am not sure that something of the externality of the old idea does not cling to the new and better statement. In any case we can escape from this external way of thinking only as we realize in thought and act that democracy is a *personal* way of individual life; that it signifies the possession and continual use of certain attitudes, forming personal character and determining desire and purpose in all the relations of life. Instead of thinking of our own dispositions and habits as accommodated to certain institutions we have to learn to think of the latter as expressions, projections, and extensions of habitually dominant personal attitudes.

Democracy as a personal, an individual, way of life involves nothing fundamentally new. But when applied it puts a new practical meaning in old ideas. Put into effect it signifies that powerful present enemies of democracy can be successfully met only by the creation of personal attitudes in individual human beings; that we must get over our tendency to think that its defense can be found in any external means whatever, whether military or civil, if they are separated from individual attitudes so deep-seated as to constitute personal character.

Democracy is a way of life controlled by a working faith in the possibilities of human nature. Belief in the Common Man is a familiar article in the democratic creed. That belief is without basis and significance save as it means faith in the potentialities of human nature as that nature is exhibited in every human being irrespective of race, color, sex, birth, and family, of material or cultural wealth. This faith may be enacted in statutes, but it is only on paper unless it is put in force in the attitudes which human beings display to one another in all the incidents and relations of daily life. To denounce Naziism for intolerance, cruelty and stimulation of hatred amounts to fostering insincerity if, in our personal relations to other persons, if, in our daily walk and conversation, we are moved by racial, color, or other class prejudice; indeed, by anything save a generous belief in their possibilities as human beings, a belief which brings with it the need for providing conditions which will enable these capacities to reach fulfillment. The democratic faith in human equality is belief that every human being, independent of the quantity or range of his personal endowment, has the right to equal opportunity with every other person for development of whatever gifts he has. The democratic belief in the principle of leadership is a generous one. It is universal. It is belief in the capacity of every person to lead his own life free from coercion and imposition by others provided right conditions are supplied.

Democracy is a way of personal life controlled not merely by faith in human nature in general but by faith in the capacity of human beings for intelligent judgment and action if proper conditions are furnished. I have been accused more than once and from opposed quarters of an undue, a utopian, faith in the possibilities of intelligence and in education as a correlate of intelligence. At all events, I did not invent this faith. I acquired it from my surroundings as far as those surroundings were animated by the democratic spirit. For what is the faith of democracy in the rôle of consultation, of conference, of persuasion, of discussion, in formation of public opinion, which in the long run is self-corrective, except faith in the capacity of the intelligence of the common man to respond with common sense to the free play of facts and ideas which are secured by effective guarantees of free inquiry, free assembly, and free communication? I am willing to leave to upholders of totalitarian states of the right and the left the view that faith in the capacities of intelligence is utopian. For the faith is so deeply embedded in the methods which are intrinsic to democracy that when a professed democrat denies the faith he convicts himself of treachery to his profession.

When I think of the conditions under which men and women are living in many foreign countries today, fear of espionage, with danger hanging over the meeting of friends for friendly conversation in private gatherings, I am inclined to believe that the heart and final guarantee of democracy is in free gatherings of neighbors on the street corner to discuss back and forth what is read in uncensored news of the day, and in gatherings of friends in the living rooms of houses and apartments to converse freely with one another. Intolerance, abuse, calling of names because of differences of opinion about religion or politics or business, as well as because of differences of race, color, wealth, or degree of culture, are treason to the democratic way of life. For everything which bars freedom and fullness of communication sets up barriers that divide human beings into sets and cliques, into antagonistic sects and factions, and thereby undermines the democratic way of life. Merely legal guarantees of the civil liberties of free belief, free expression, free assembly are of little avail if in daily life freedom of communication, the give and take of ideas, facts, experiences, is choked by mutual suspicion, by abuse, by fear and hatred. These things destroy the essential condition of the democratic way of living even more effectually than open coercion, which—as the example of totalitarian states proves—is effective only when it succeeds in breeding hate, suspicion, intolerance in the minds of individual human beings.

Finally, given the two conditions just mentioned, democracy as a way of life is controlled by personal faith in personal day-by-day working together with others. Democracy is the belief that even when needs and ends or consequences are different for each individual, the habit of amicable co-operation—which may include, as in sport, rivalry and competition—is itself a priceless addition to life. To take as far as possible every conflict which arises—and they are bound to arise—out of the atmosphere and medium of force, of violence as a means of settlement, into that of discussion and of intelligence, is to treat those who disagree—even profoundly—with us as those from whom we may learn, and in so far, as friends. A genuinely democratic faith in peace is faith in the possibility of conducting disputes, controversies, and conflicts as co-operative undertakings in which both parties learn by giving the other a chance to express itself, instead of having one party conquer by forceful suppression of the other—a suppression which is none the less one of violence when it takes place by psychological means of ridicule, abuse, intimidation, instead of by overt imprisonment or in concentration camps. To co-operate by giving differences a chance to show themselves because of the belief that the expression of difference is not only a right of the other persons but is a means of enriching one's own life-experience, is inherent in the democratic personal way of life.

If what has been said is charged with being a set of moral commonplaces, my only reply is that that is just the point in saying them. For to get rid of the habit of thinking of democracy as something institutional and external and to acquire the habit of treating it as a way of personal life is to realize that democracy is a moral ideal and so far as it becomes a fact is a moral fact. It is to realize that democracy is a reality only as it is indeed a commonplace of living.

Since my adult years have been given to the pursuit of philosophy, I shall ask your indulgence if in concluding I state briefly the democratic faith in the formal terms of a philosophic position. So stated, democracy is belief in the ability of human experience to generate the aims and methods by which further experience will grow in ordered richness. Every other form of moral and social faith rests upon the idea that experience must be subjected at some point or other to some form of external control; to some "authority" alleged to exist outside the processes of experience. Democracy is the faith that the process of experience is more important than any special result attained, so that special results achieved are of ultimate value only as they are used to enrich and order the ongoing process. Since the process of experience is capable of being educative, faith in democracy is all one with faith in experience and education. All ends and values that are cut off from the ongoing process become arrests, fixations. They strive to fixate what has been gained instead of using it to open the road and point the way to new and better experiences.

If one asks what is meant by experience in this connection, my reply is that it is that free interaction of individual human beings with surrounding conditions, especially the human surroundings, which develops and satisfies need and desire by increasing knowledge of things as they are. Knowledge of conditions as they are is the only solid ground for communication and sharing; all other communication means the subjection of some persons to the personal opinion of other persons. Need and desire—out of which grow purpose and direction of energy—go beyond what exists, and hence beyond knowledge, beyond science. They continually open the way into the unexplored and unattained future.

Democracy as compared with other ways of life is the sole way of living which believes wholeheartedly in the process of experience as end and as means; as that which is capable of generating the science which is the sole dependable authority for the direction of further experience and which releases emotions, needs, and desires so as to call into being the things that have not existed in the past. For every way of life that fails in its democracy limits the contacts, the exchanges, the communications, the interactions by which experience is steadied while it is also enlarged and enriched. The task of this release and enrichment is one that has to be carried on day by day. Since it is one that can have no end till experience itself comes to an end, the task of democracy is forever that of creation of a freer and more humane experience in which all share and to which all contribute.

Notes

CHAPTER 2

1. Mill's *Utility of Religion* contains a sustained treatment of the power of public opinion. It was written while *On Liberty* (1859) was being composed, but not published until 1874, one year after Mill's death.

2. The first few pages of *Utility of Religion* (1874/1958a) sketch an argument for the inseparability of truth and utility. In *On Liberty* Mill does not distinguish between truth and knowledge; so I have not done so in my analysis. Mill would more properly use 'knowledge' than 'truth'.

3. Philosophical rationalists also resorted to subjective criteria for truth, claiming, e.g., that if an idea is clear and distinct, it is true.

4. See, for example, Peirce's essay, ''The Fixation of Belief'' (1877). Widely reprinted. See esp. Vol. 5, *Collected Papers of Charles Sanders Peirce*, paragraphs 358–87, edited by Charles Hartshorne and Paul Weiss (1934).

5. Mill is mistaken to conclude that anyone who denies to others the opportunity to hear an argument assumes his own infallibility. One might only assume (a) that the excluded group is so unfit to judge the question that they would be harmed, or would do harm, if exposed to it, and (b) that he is much better fitted to judge than they. An assumption of marked superiority is not necessarily an assumption of infallibility. Mill later defines the assumption of infallibility as precisely the forbidding to others of the opportunity to judge a question for themselves; i.e., ''infallible'' *means* forbidding inquiry. When someone assumes infallibility in the first (and conventional) sense, then it can be decisively argued that no one is infallible. When ''infallible'' is taken in the second sense, then Mill must argue that such censorship is injurious; and this is just what he does.

6. Mill was not a Christian, but he admired much in the teachings of Jesus.

7. No doubt the most widely read and studied critique of utilitarianism in recent years is that found in *A Theory of Justice*, by John Rawls (1971). An ex-

ceptionally sophisticated characterization and defense of utilitarianism was recently presented by R. M. Hare in *Moral Thinking* (1981).

8. The last clause is a reference to the qualitative test of value.

9. The tension between a sort of absolutism and a sort of experimentalism exists not only between *On Liberty* and *Utilitarianism*. It is within *On Liberty* itself. It is found in respect to the status of the principle of utility; and it also appears in connection with the principle of liberty enunciated in chapter I. There Mill says the principle is entitled to govern "absolutely" the limits of authority over the individual. The Mill of chapter II frowns on such expressions. (See note to Appendix A for a brief account of the principle of liberty.)

10. The theory of the social contract has more credibility when one assumes the conception of reason prevailing in the seventeenth and eighteenth centuries, according to which the rational conclusions reached in the thought of any rational being must be identical to the rational conclusions of any other rational being.

CHAPTER 3

1. For Mill's sustained analyses, see *A System of Logic* (1872/1956), Bk. I, Ch. III; and *An Examination of Sir William Hamiltons's Philosophy* (1865/1979), Chs. XI and XII, with Appendix to Ch. XII.

2. See Mill's edition of James Mill, *Analysis of the Phenomena of the Human Mind* (1869), where he adds many explanatory remarks and some critical notes to what was then regarded as the definitive account of the associationist theory.

3. For a brief and excellent analysis of the difficulties in Mill's union of logic and associationism, see Ernest Nagel's introduction to *John Stuart Mill's Philosophy of Scientific Method* (Nagel, 1950).

4. Dewey's views were profoundly influenced by the biological theory of Charles Darwin, which held that variations in living organisms are due to natural selection, as life forms contend with variations in their respective environments. Peirce and James had made fertile use of Darwin before Dewey, and Dewey built on their work. In "The Fixation of Belief" (1877) Peirce had said that all ideas are "habits of action." James said in *The Principles of Psychology* (1890) that mind is "a fighter for ends."

5. Dewey always insists that the meaning of an event is "in the future"—in the functions of that event in future interactions. It is not clear why he must hold inflexibly to this assumption. If we abandon the traditional notions of substance and essence, then meaning consists in relations, but not exclusively in forthcoming relations. Why cannot the meaning of steel and coffee, for example, consist in part in the antecedent conditions that bring them into being? We know better what steel and coffee are when we know the relations upon which their existence depends. A pragmatist can acknowledge this much while still drawing attention to the ways that ideas are deliberate anticipations of the future.

6. See Bk. III, Chs. VI–X in *A System of Logic* for Mill's methods of inquiry.

7. In various writings, however, Mill repeated his point about the importance for individual intellectual development of participating in intelligent controversy.

8. Dewey does not mention that Mill also argued much to this effect; nor does he seem to recognize how far Mill progressed toward the idea of social intelligence.

CHAPTER 4

1. I have edited this passage to make it conform to contemporary usage.

2. Locke himself introduced a rudimentary form of associationist psychology. It is not instrumental in either his political or pedagogical theory.

3. The family precedes the social contract; but marriage, too, is a contract in Locke's view. While the family is a necessary condition of life, it does not shape human faculties, but aids in the stimulation of their development.

4. See p. 17 of this volume for illustrative quotations.

5. There is rather little scholarship on Mill's philosophy of education. The only systematic study of which I am aware is Francis W. Garforth's *Educative Democracy: John Stuart Mill on Education and Society* (1980). He quotes many of Mill's statements about education, but he does not interpret them for their presuppositions about human nature. He takes for granted that Mill's educational thought is predicated throughout on associationist psychology. John Gray's *Mill on Liberty: A Defence* (1983) notes the ambiguities in Mill's philosophical anthropology (seeing Mill more as a romantic than a Lockean), but his work is not addressed to Mill's educational theory.

6. In his perfectly liberal moods, Mill does not sound unlike his father, who, Mill reports, had a sublime confidence in the effects of universal literacy, freedom of speech, and popular government (1873/1957a). The elder Mill had by no means separated himself from Locke's heritage either.

7. A recent book amply documents Mill's deep concern with virtue, but it does not address the issue of how, according to Mill, we become virtuous (Semmel, 1984).

CHAPTER 5

1. Mill refuted this view in *Principles of Political Economy* (1871/1965). Dewey does not mention Mill's discussion of this issue.

2. See especially *Experience and Nature* (Dewey, 1925a), Ch. 1 in both the first and revised editions.

3. The ideas expressed succinctly in "Three Independent Factors in Morals" are presented a bit obscurely and at greater length in the *Ethics* (Dewey & Tufts, 1932).

4. I remarked in chapter 2 that Mill's ethical theory is better understood if we do not insist on pressing it into a utilitarian mold, as he himself did. His attempt to be sensitive to the varieties of moral experience made his utilitarianism virtually disappear as the exclusive test of morality. Two recent

studies of Mill regard him as a utilitarian, yet they reconstruct the meaning of utilitarianism to display some of Mill's moral sensitivity. They are John Gray's *Mill on Liberty: A Defence* (1983) and Fred R. Berger's *Happiness, Justice, and Freedom* (1984).

5. An overly compendious but nevertheless valuable account of Dewey's contributions to controversies regarding public policy has been provided by Gary Bullert in *The Politics of John Dewey* (1983).

6. One might add R. M. Hare's *Moral Thinking* (1981). Hare's theory is also a form of absolutism, for it contains the view that all valid moral criteria are reducible to claims of utility.

Jürgen Habermas is a widely read and influential moral philosopher, and his approach seems to be distinctly different from those of the writers listed above. In a series of books starting with *Knowledge and Human Interest* (1971), he has defended the thesis that moral controversy should be decided by free and equal communication. He has had much to say about the nature and conditions of such communication. All this sounds much like Mill and Dewey. Habermas, however, insists that there cannot be undistorted communication until all forms of illegitimate power have been eradicated. To him, this means that discourse in a capitalist economy must be distorted; so debates within the culture of private enterprise are inherently invalid. The relative merits of economic systems are eminently debatable, but Habermas excludes this debate from legitimacy. Both Dewey and Mill had strong sympathies for versions of socialism, but neither would take the drastic step of wholesale rejection of a discussion of economic systems in a context that is other than socialistic. In Mill's terms, Habermas seems to have adopted a stance of infallibility. In Dewey's terms, we might very well add that Habermas has failed to respect conclusions other than his own. A suspicious person, such as myself, is apt to think that Habermas has a hidden agenda. It may be that his commitment to a version of social intelligence is not as strong as his commitment to socialism; perhaps his particular theory of communicative competence is a Trojan horse. It must be conceded, nevertheless, that Habermas's writings frequently show great insight into the nature and conditions of effective communication. *The Legitimation Crisis* (1975) or *Communication and the Evolution of Society* (1979) might well be consulted in this context.

An apparent convert to pragmatism, Richard Rorty is another author who seems to resemble Dewey. He wants all controversy to be addressed by means of what he calls conversation. Rorty's "conversation," however, is unable to gird itself with any intellectual authority. In contradiction to Dewey, he refuses to recognize any cognitive validity in science or scientific method, or in anything else. See *Philosophy and the Mirror of Nature* (Rorty, 1979) and *Consequences of Pragmatism* (Rorty, 1982).

7. The most important of these interpretations is Morton White's "Value and Obligation in Dewey and Lewis" (1949b). See also Ch. XIII of his *Social Thought in America* (1949a). My response to White is "Dewey's Theory of Moral Deliberation" (1978).

8. The *Ethics* was a collaboration of Dewey and Tufts. The pages cited, however, were written by Dewey.

CHAPTER 6

1. This is not to say that association has no part in human nature. Learning requires associative processes. It is the reduction of all behavior to association that is dead. Likewise, both sensationalism and subjectivism are no longer tenable.

APPENDIX A

1. Passing by Mill's qualifications to it, the principle declares that no one has the right to interfere in that conduct of an individual that has no direct effects on others. When there are direct consequences for others, interference is justified only to prevent harm to them. It is not clear that it would be invariably consistent with utility to permit persons to do as they wish so long as they cause no direct injury to others. (As noted in note no. 9 to chapter 2, Mill's claims for the unqualified validity of this principle are inconsistent with his experimentalism.) Mill's distinction between self-regarding and other-regarding behavior is meant to be decisive. He seems to believe that the category of self-regarding conduct encompasses a large and significant domain of activity. The distinction, however, turns out to be vague, and Mill himself has difficulty applying it. The range of distinctively self-regarding conduct appears actually to diminish to the vanishing point. (It is further evidence of Mill's Lockean propensities that he attempts to accomplish with the self-regarding/other-regarding distinction what Locke intended to accomplish with his doctrine of natural rights. He wants to circumscribe a permanent domain of activity that shall be free of all interference.)

APPENDIX B

1. Dewey's strong stands on social issues are properly regarded as proposals, hypotheses for action. He was not dictating them to his fellow citizens, but submitting them to the process of social intelligence.

2. *The Quest For Certainty* (1929), selections from pp. 54–55, 57–59, 68–70, 80–81, 91–92, 132.

3. *Liberalism and Social Action* (1935/1963b), selections from pp. 28–32, 42–47, 49–50, 53–54, 67–74, 79, 93.

4. *The Public and Its Problems* (1927), selections from pp. 314, 316–17, 319, 323–24, 333–36, 339–41, 345–50, 360–61, 365–68, 371–72.

5. *Ethics* (1932), selections from pp. 328–30, 337–38. (These passages are among those written by Dewey.)

References

NOTE: The complete works of John Dewey are being published by Southern Illinois University Press, Carbondale. *The Early Works, 1882–1898,* have been published in five volumes (1967–71). *The Middle Works, 1899–1924,* have been published in fifteen volumes (1971–83). *The Later Works, 1925–53* (to be sixteen volumes) are not yet completed, but the first eight volumes have been published (1981–86). All volumes in the series are edited by Jo Ann Boydston. References to Dewey's works published prior to 1933 are taken from this edition, with abbreviated citations below to *Early Works, Middle Works,* and *Later Works.*

Berger, F. R. (1984). *Happiness, justice, and freedom.* Berkeley: University of California Press.

Bullert, G. (1983). *The politics of John Dewey.* Buffalo, NY: Prometheus Books.

Dewey, J. (1916). *Democracy and education* (*Middle works,* Vol. 9).

Dewey, J. (1917). The need for a recovery of philosophy (*Middle works,* Vol. 10, pp. 3–48).

Dewey, J. (1919). Philosophy and democracy (*Middle works,* Vol. 11, pp. 41–53).

Dewey, J. (1920). *Reconstruction in philosophy* (*Middle works,* Vol. 12, pp. 80–201).

Dewey, J. (1922a). Events and meanings (*Middle works,* Vol. 13, pp. 276–80).

Dewey, J. (1922b). *Human nature and conduct* (*Middle works,* Vol. 14).

Dewey, J. (1925a). *Experience and nature* (*Later works,* Vol. 1).

Dewey, J. (1925b). The development of American pragmatism (*Later works,* Vol. 2, pp. 3–21).

Dewey, J. (1927). *The public and its problems* (*Later works,* Vol. 2, pp. 237–372).

Dewey, J. (1929). *The quest for certainty* (*Later works,* Vol. 4).

Dewey, J. (1930a). *Individualism, old and new* (*Later works,* Vol. 5, pp. 43–123).

Dewey, J. (1930b). Three independent factors in morals (*Later works,* Vol. 5, pp. 279–88).

Dewey, J. (1940). Creative democracy—The task before us. In S. Ratner (Ed.), *The philosopher of the common man: Essays in honor of John Dewey to celebrate his eightieth birthday* (pp. 220–28). New York: G. P. Putnam's Sons.

Dewey, J. (1963a). *Freedom and culture.* New York: G. P. Putnam's Sons. (Original work published 1939)

Dewey, J. (1963b). *Liberalism and social action.* New York: G. P. Putnam's Sons. (Original work published 1935)

Dewey, J., & Tufts, J. H. (1932). *Ethics* (rev. ed.) (*Later works,* Vol. 7).

Dworkin, R. (1976). *Taking rights seriously.* Cambridge, MA: Harvard University Press.

Garforth, F. W. (1980). *Educative democracy: John Stuart Mill on education and society.* Oxford, England: Oxford University Press.

Gewirth, A. (1978). *Reason and morality.* Chicago: The University of Chicago Press.

Gouinlock, J. (1978). Dewey's theory of moral deliberation. *Ethics, 88*(3), 218–228.

Gray, J. (1983). *Mill on liberty: A defence.* London: Routledge and Kegan Paul.

Green, T. H., & Grose, T. H. (Eds.). (1964). *David Hume: Philosophical works* (4 vols.). Aalen, West Germany: Scientia Verlag. (Original work published 1886)

Habermas, J. (1971). *Knowledge and human interest* (J. J. Shapiro, Trans.). Boston: Beacon Press.

Habermas, J. (1975). *The legitimation crisis* (T. McCarthy, Trans.). Boston: Beacon Press.

Habermas, J. (1979). *Communication and the evolution of society* (T. McCarthy, Trans.). Boston: Beacon Press.

Hare, R. M. (1981). *Moral thinking.* Oxford, England: Oxford University Press.

Hartshorne, C., & Weiss, P. (Eds.). (1934). *Collected papers of Charles Sanders Peirce* (Vol. 5). Cambridge, MA: Harvard University Press.

James, W. (1890). *The principles of psychology* (2 vols.). New York: Henry Holt.

Locke, J. (1958). *An essay concerning human understanding* (4th ed., 2 vols.). (A. C. Fraser, Ed.). New York: Dover Press. (Original 4th ed. published 1700)

Locke, J. (1960). *Second treatise of government.* In J. Locke, *Two treatises of government* (Peter Laslett, Ed.). Cambridge, England: Cambridge University Press. (Original work published 1690)

Locke, J. (1966). *Of the conduct of the understanding.* (F. W. Garforth, Ed.). New York: Teachers College Press. (Original work published 1706)

Locke, J. (1968). *Some thoughts concerning education.* In J. L. Axtell (Ed.), *The educational writings of John Locke* (pp. 111–325). Cambridge, England: Cambridge University Press. (Original work published 1693)

MacIntyre, A. (1984). *After virtue* (2nd ed.). Notre Dame, IN: University of Notre Dame Press.

Mill, J. S. (Ed.). (1869). *Analysis of the phenomena of the human mind* (2 vols.), by James Mill. A new edition, with illustrative and critical notes by A. Bain, A. Findlater, & G. Grote, and with additional notes by J. S. Mill. London: Longmans, Green, Reader and Dyer.

Mill, J. S. (1956). *A system of logic, ratiocinative and inductive* (8th ed.). London: Longmans, Green. (Original 8th ed. published 1872)

Mill, J. S. (1957a). *Autobiography* (C. V. Shields, Ed.). New York: Liberal Arts Press. (Original work published 1873)

Mill, J. S. (1957b). *Utilitarianism.* (O. Piest, Ed.). Indianapolis: Bobbs-Merrill. (Original work published 1863)

Mill, J. S. (1958a). *Nature and utility of religion* (G. Nakhnikian, Ed.). Indianapolis: Bobbs-Merrill. (Original work published 1874 as the first two parts of *Nature, the utility of religion, theism, being three essays on religion*)

Mill, J. S. (1958b). *Considerations on representative government* (C. V. Shields, Ed.). Indianapolis: Bobbs-Merrill. (Original work published 1861)

Mill, J. S. (1961). *Auguste Comte and positivism.* Ann Arbor: The University of Michigan Press. (Original work published 1865)

Mill, J. S. (1965). *Principles of political economy* (7th ed.). Vol. III of J. M. Robson (Ed.), *Collected works of John Stuart Mill.* Toronto: The University of Toronto Press. London: Routledge and Kegan Paul. (Original 7th ed. published 1871)

Mill, J. S. (1978). *On liberty* (E. Rapaport, Ed.). Indianapolis: Hackett Publishing Company. (Original work published 1859)

Mill, J. S. (1979). *An examination of Sir William Hamilton's philosophy.* Vol. IX of J. M. Robson (Ed.), *Collected works of John Stuart Mill.* Toronto: The University of Toronto Press. London: Routledge and Kegan Paul. (Original work published 1865)

Nagel, E. (Ed.). (1950). *John Stuart Mill's philosophy of scientific method.* New York: Hafner.

Nozick, R. (1974). *Anarchy, state, and utopia.* New York: Basic Books.

Peirce, C. S. (1877). The fixation of belief. *Popular Science Monthly, 12* (Nov.), 1–15.

Rawls, J. (1971). *A theory of justice.* Cambridge, MA: Harvard University Press.

Rorty, R. (1979). *Philosophy and the mirror of nature.* Princeton, NJ: Princeton University Press.

Rorty, R. (1982). *Consequences of pragmatism.* Minneapolis: University of Minnesota Press.

Semmel, B. (1984). *John Stuart Mill and the pursuit of virtue.* New Haven, CT: Yale University Press.

White, M. (1949a). *Social thought in America.* New York: Viking.

White, M. (1949b). Value and obligation in Dewey and Lewis. *Philosophical Review, 58*(4), 321–330.

Further Scholarly Resources

The most complete bibliography of the writings of John Stuart Mill is *Bibliography of the Published Writings of John Stuart Mill*, edited by N. MacMinn, J. R. Hainds, and J. McCrimmon (Evanston: Northwestern University Press, 1945). This source is supplemented by the *Mill News Letter*, edited by J. M. Robson and published semi-annually by the University of Toronto Press. The *News Letter* also provides a guide to secondary literature. The University of Toronto Press is publishing the complete works of Mill: *Collected Works of John Stuart Mill* (1965–), edited by J. M. Robson.

The best bibliography of writings by and about John Dewey is *John Dewey: A Centennial Bibliography*, by Milton Halsey Thomas (Chicago: The University of Chicago Press, 1962). Southern Illinois University Press publishes *Checklist of Writings about John Dewey, 1887–1977* (2nd ed., enlarged), edited by Jo Ann Boydston. Also useful to scholars and students is *Guide to the Works of John Dewey*, edited by Jo Ann Boydston (Carbondale: Southern Illinois University Press, 1970). This volume addresses various areas of Dewey's philosophy. In each instance an essay and a relevant bibliography is provided by a distinguished scholar.

Index

Absolutism
  and democracy, 77, 145–46
  and education, 141
  in Mill, 154n
  and moral disagreement, 65, 66
  in morals, 54, 60, 63, 77
  opposed to social intelligence, 64
Aesthetic attitude, in knowing, 115–16
Affirmative action, 13
Altruism, 27, 46–47, 48, 49
Analysis
  and association of ideas, 46
  as method of inquiry, 26, 122, 127
Antoninus, Marcus Aurelius, 11, 91, 92–94
Aristotle, 1, 68, 91
Association of ideas, 25–26, 28, 124, 154n, 155n, 157n
  and analysis, 46
  and culture, 42, 43
  Dewey's criticism of, 39, 41, 42, 75
  in education, 37–38, 45–46, 48–49, 155n
  laws of, 27
  theory of motivation, 27–28
Authority
  in classic tradition, 54, 62
  collective, 85
  as custom, 85–86
  as dogmatic, 145
  as expertise, 16, 59
  opposed to democracy, 53, 121
  as protection from criticism, 89
  of public opinion, 85, 149
  as scientific, 113

  as silencer of opinion, 85
  threatened by freedom of speech, 18

Bacon, Francis, 130
Bentham, Jeremy, 20, 21, 76, 124, 130
Berger, Fred R., 156n
Bullert, Gary, 156n

Carlyle, Thomas, 38
Censorship
  evils of, 84–85
  by government, 10, 84
  as impediment to knowledge, 10
  and infallibility, 11, 91, 153n
  and intelligence, 11–12, 13–14
  and obedience, 16
  by society, 10, 84
Change
  in classic tradition, 54
  Dewey's emphasis on, 54
  in liberalism, 122, 123, 126–27
  and moral commitment, 55
  and science, 114–16
Cicero, Marcus Tullius, 98
Classic tradition, 54, 55, 57, 64
  difficulties in, 54
  justifying inequality, 56
Coleridge, Samuel Taylor, 38
Communication. *See also* Democracy; Discourse; Freedom of communication; Social intelligence
  by artists, 72, 121, 140–41
  in capitalistic environment, 156n
  as criticism, 52, 103

ABOUT THE AUTHOR

James Gouinlock has been teaching in the Department of Philosophy at Emory University since 1971. Before that he taught at the State University of New York at Buffalo and at DePauw University. His undergraduate studies took place at Cornell, and he received his Ph.D. in Philosophy from Columbia University in 1969. His teaching interests cover every facet of moral philosophy. He also teaches classic American philosophy and philosophy of education. Rather than deluge students with multitudes of fact, Professor Gouinlock emphasizes the mastery of crucial concepts and the use of critical skills. He has found that the quality of classroom experience is of first importance in making philosophy a vital part of liberal education.

While Dr. Gouinlock's scholarly publications have attended to a variety of philosophic subjects, his writings are principally in the field of American philosophy, especially the philosophy of John Dewey. He is the author, for example, of *John Dewey's Philosophy of Value* (New York: Humanities Press, 1972) and editor of *The Moral Writings of John Dewey* (New York: Hafner Press, 1976). He has served both as Director of Graduate Studies in Philosophy and as Chairman of the Philosophy Department at Emory. He was on the Executive Committee of the Society for the Advancement of American Philosophy and was President of the Society from 1983 to 1986.